# AM I A REAL CHRISTIAN?

# AM I A REAL CHRISTIAN?

## RANDRICK CHANCE

Copyright 2012
Randrick Chance

All rights reserved
Printed in the USA

Strategic Secrets, LLC.
P.O. Box 11942
Huntsville, AL 35814
www.strategicsecrets.com

www.amiarealchristian.com

Edited by Jolena King

Unless otherwise stated, all Scripture texts are taken from the King James Version (KJV). Italics and bold not found in original quotations are used for emphasis. Parentheses ( ) denote supplied words or explanation. Other versions used are The Clear Word (TCW), Bible in Basic English (BBE), and God's Word (GW).

ISBN - 13: 978-0-9843951-1-8 (paperback)
ISBN - 10: 0-9843951-1-3

ISBN - 13: 978-0-9843951-5-6 (ePub)
ISBN - 10: 0-9843951-5-6

# CONTENTS

Introduction ................................................................... 7
A Striking Dichotomy ...................................................... 10
Will the Real Christian Please Stand Up? ...................... 12
The Root Problem of Just *"Knowing"* ............................ 31
Cures for Mediocre Christianity ..................................... 45
- **Cure #1**: Remember Who You Are
  and Whose You Are ...................................... 50
- **Cure #2**: Depend on Christ
  and the Holy Spirit ....................................... 56
- **Cure #3**: Surrender the Fight ............................. 62
  - Action 1: Put on God's Armor
  - Action 2: Cling to the Vine
  - Action 3: Be a Sheep—A Real Sheep
- **Cure #4**: Claim God's Promises .......................... 69
  - Faith; Forgiveness; Strength; Peace
  - Protection; Provision; Success
- **Cure #5**: Use God's Seven-Step Plan for Victory ..... 78
  - Choose Not to Sin
  - Keep the Faith
  - Make No Provision for the Flesh
  - Consider Yourself Dead to Sin
  - Claim the Victory and Power in Christ
  - Take God's Exit Plan
  - Ask for Help
- **Cure #6**: Be Transformed by Renewing Your Mind.. 81
  - Fill Your Mind with the Knowledge of God
  - Meditate Daily on God's Words

- Practice the Teachings of God
- Memorize the Word of God
- Speak and Sing the Word of God
- Subject Every Thought to the Word of God
- Change the Quality of Your Information
- **Cure #7**: Apply the Discipline of Action (Strategy Secrets) ...... 91
  - 1. Ask God for Power and Wisdom to Be Disciplined
  - 2. Exercise Full Control of Your Will
  - 3. Learn More and You Will Be More
  - 4. Just Do It.
  - 5. Teach your Heart and Lips to Praise and Thank God
  - 6. Establish a Daily Success Routine
  - 7. Never, Never, Never Give Up
- Bonus Cure for Mediocre Christianity ...... 99

Reflection Notes ...... 104

Recommended Resources ...... 110

# INTRODUCTION

*Examine yourselves to see whether you are still in the Christian faith. Test yourselves! Don't you recognize that you are people in whom Jesus Christ lives? Could it be that you're failing the test?*
2 Corinthians 13:5 (GW)

A couple of years ago, the above text and scores of others convinced me that the Christian life is no joke. It's not as "easy" as some preachers might teach. This Christian journey is truly a battle, which requires constant spiritual warfare. (See Ephesians 6:12; 2 Timothy 2:3-4; and 1 Peter 5:8-9).

It is apparent that God expects more of His children than simple acceptance of His marvelous gift of grace. He wants us to GROW in grace. He wants us to become like *Him*! (2 Peter 3:18; 1 John 3:1-3; Colossians 3:1-10)

The spiritual plateau I had hit seemed to prevent my growing more like Christ. So I decided to do what most Christians do when they find themselves in a spiritual dilemma – I settled for average, second-rate Christianity. I accepted mediocrity, still professing to be a born-again Christian, talking "the talk."

Then I came across 2 Corinthians 13:1-10. It made me face myself squarely as a man of God, honestly examining every facet of my spiritual life, I had to ask myself, *"Am I a Real Christian?"* Mind you, at this time, I'd been a full-time missionary, preached in the US and overseas, could hold my own in a theological debate, appeared on TV, published in

Christian magazines, and a host of other religious niceties. You might say I was a "professional" Christian.

But do you know what? None of those things impress God. The Holy Spirit pierced my heart and led me to take a closer look at the teachings of Jesus. When I asked myself the sobering question, *Am I a Real Christian?* I had to admit, I did not measure up well at all. I was missing the mark, not by a few inches or yards, but by furlongs and miles.

Truth be told, I really wasn't following all the light of the Truth I knew. Sure, I didn't engage in reckless acts and "big" sins but there were those "darling" sins. You know what I mean? Those things that preachers don't talk about, like: pride, "tiny" dishonesties, tantrums, "Christian" curse words, neglect of duties, laziness, bitterness, an unforgiving spirit, gossip, slander, murmuring, complaining, sowing seeds of discord, criticism, half-hearted service, indifference, selfishness, etc.—things that make you say, "Hmmm."

Yes, I know that we must look to Jesus and not at self when it comes to salvation. He is, indeed, our "All in all." Yet I grew weary of living a mediocre Christian life. It is discouraging to only win an occasional skirmish, but lose most of the battles, when God's plan is for us to be victorious gladiators in *His* strength—from victory to victory! I had bought into the popular crutch-song, "*We fall down but we get up,*" as though it were real gospel. That song fails to elevate the full power of Jesus to not only save us from sin but to transform us from sinners to saints. (Hebrews 7:25; 1 John 1:9; Jude 1:24-25)

After my spiritual check up and much searching of scripture, a favorable diagnosis emerged that eventually became a sermon—to myself. I preached that message over and over to myself, even recording it on an MP3 player. After a time, I accidentally deleted it, but—praise God!—those notes were still in one of my Bibles.

A few months ago I revisited that message. I could see fellow Christian soldiers reverting to the same levels of mediocrity that I had engaged in. I thought, *There's so much more to living for God than a few paltry victories every now and again. We must stop excusing ourselves for low-to-average living, blaming everything and everyone else for why we "fall" into sin and just can't seem to overcome.*

I sat down and searched the Scriptures diligently for answers. Soon a full sermon series came to life, which has now become this book. I hope you'll experience a holy transformation as you come under the surgical two-edged sword of God's Word.

Brace yourself. This assessment will not be easy but it is necessary to enter your next chapter of victorious Christian living. Start turning the pages and begin your own spiritual check up. Proven prescriptions from God's word are presented to treat any malady you may have. May God richly bless you as you seek to know and reflect *His* character more and more.

A fellow pilgrim,
"Chance"

# A STRIKING DICHOTOMY

A dichotomy exists between Eastern and Western cultures, between Liberals and Conservatives, between the secular mind and the Christian mind. We recognize that. But there's also a striking dichotomy between Christians!—*real* Christians and *professed* Christians.

One group reflects the life of Christ by their words, actions, and even their thoughts. Another group *profess* to know God and *claim* to be born again, yet their actions betray them. This, sadly, seems to reflect the larger group of believers today.

Most lay people do not have advanced degrees, but they surely are good "professors." They *profess* that they are living a Christian life. They profess acquaintance with God and His character. They even profess to be sanctified, Holy Ghost filled, water-baptized, and on their way to heaven. But are they? Are they (am I) fit and ready for heaven?

The question you need to ask yourself right now is, "Am I a Real Christian?" This book is going to challenge you, rock you, maybe shock you, but hopefully awaken you. You and I must be honest enough to ask: **Am I a Real Christian?**

In these pages we'll examine the difference between *Knowing and Doing,* and what it really means to *BE* a Christian. "The ROOT Problem of Just *'Knowing'*" uncovers the reason we have a problem. We'll also explore WHY most Christians are living on the low-to-average plains of life.

Then we'll delve into the **CURES** for *mediocre* Christianity. We'll unravel the dichotomy between being a *real* Christian and simply *professing* to be a Christian. We'll discuss how to not only *know* what is good for us, but even more importantly, how to *do* the good we know, as well as *when* we ought to do it. We can do all things through Christ, Who strengthens us (Philippians 4:13).

> "Thanks be to God for His unspeakable gift" (2 Corinthians 9:15)!

# WILL THE *REAL* CHRISTIAN PLEASE STAND UP?

Let's make a distinction right from the start. This book is called *Am I a Real Christian?* It's not written for those who are clearly not Christians. It's for the so-called "born again," "Holy Ghost filled," "water-baptized" believer in Christ. The one who *says* he or she knows God. It's a diagnostic test for you and me.

Also, when we talk of following God's commands, we're talking about all His immutable instructions, teachings, guidelines, and principles—not just the Ten Commandments. Some people don't realize or take into consideration that whatever God asks us to do or not do are commands and should be carried out—with His power. For example: judge not, love one another, forgive, be angry and sin not, etc.

Now that we've settled that, let me ask you a heart-to-heart question: Are you a Christian? How do you know you are a *TRUE* Christian? I have no doubt that you know *of* Christ and maybe even serve in church or go on missions. But "Are you a real Christian?"

Can people tell that you are a child of God when they look at you? Will your co-workers, friends, wife, husband, or children say that you are a Christian? **Will the REAL Christian please stand up?**

Some of us are "good" Christians in public, but act like demons at home! You *can* fool people, though not for too long, but you certainly can't fool God. The Bible is the litmus test to find out if you are the REAL deal or a FAKE—an imposter. The answer may challenge and rock you to the core.

The biggest breakdown in modern education today is that there are plenty of KNOWERS, but few DOERS. There's much learning, much theory, but little, if any, practical application. Thus we have a lot of people who know many things, yet are still uneducated. They have book knowledge but no experiential knowledge.

You've heard the saying "Knowledge is power." But I beg to differ. Knowledge is *not* power! Knowledge is only **potential** power. Think about it. Almost everyone knows that smoking is bad for you, yet many highly educated people still smoke—slowly killing themselves. Even medical doctors are addicted to smoking.

Most people know that pre-marital, unprotected sex is dangerous. Yet many people cannot control their sex drives. So, knowledge is *not* power. *Knowledge* is only ***potential*** *power.*

What is power then? *Applied* knowledge is true power. It is only when you APPLY knowledge that you are powerful. When knowledge is applied, power is experienced.

The problem with Christianity today is that many people know *about* Christ and His teachings but very few live or practice those teachings. Many Christians are *professors* who *"profess"* Christ with their lips and even teach His words, but *deny* Him by the way they live because they fail to implement what Jesus taught.

That's why Christ said in Matthew 7:21 (GW), "Not everyone who says to me, 'Lord, Lord!' will enter the kingdom of heaven, but *only the person who does* what my Father in heaven wants."

He also said in Luke 6:46 (BBE), "Why do you say to me, 'Lord, Lord,' and *do not* the things which I say (teach)?"

The prophet Isaiah echoed Christ's words in Isaiah 29:13, 15, GW, "These people *worship me with their mouths* and *honor me with their lips*. But *their hearts are far from me*, and their worship of me is based on rules made by humans. How horrible it will be for those who try to hide their plans from the Lord. Their deeds are done in the dark, and they say, 'No one can see us' and 'No one can recognize us.'"

My friend, this message is a spiritual check up—a dipstick to measure the current level of your spiritual oil reservoir. In **2 Corinthians 13:5-6**, the Apostle Paul advises, "Examine yourselves, whether ye be in the faith; prove your own selves. Know ye not your own selves, how that Jesus Christ is in you, except ye be reprobates? But I trust that ye shall know that we are not reprobates."

Most of us get regular dental and medical checkups, but fail to engage in regular, consistent *spiritual* checkups. Paul wants to make sure you have not deceived yourself into *thinking* you're the real deal when in fact you might be a counterfeit.

Christ's return is imminent and we need to get serious. We don't need to be *getting ready;* we need to **BE READY**—at all times. So, how can you be *sure* you are a Christian? The only way to know is by the Bible and *the Bible only*—your bastion of Truth.

Lay aside opinions and personal preferences for now and let the Bible be our guide. Then we'll see how we measure up according to it – not according to our individual creeds or what others have told us. What we need now is a clear "Thus saith the Lord."

Let's go to James 1:22 which says, "But be ye *doers* of the word, and not *hearers only*, **deceiving** your own selves." Honestly speaking, are you a *doer* of the Word or are you a *hearer* only? Simply hearing or knowing what God requires is not enough. We must move beyond knowing and hearing, to doing.

Verse 25 continues, "But whoso looketh into the perfect law of liberty, and **continueth** therein, he being *not a forgetful hearer,* but **a doer** of the work, this man shall be **blessed** in his deed."

The blessings come as a result of *doing*, not only from hearing. Most of us hear. We read and know much, but we fail at the most important part—**DOING**—applying or practicing what we learn by reading.

**RELIGION** is not simply knowing God or knowing about God. Religion is lived out in ACTION. Look at verse 27, "Pure religion and undefiled before God and the Father is this, To visit the fatherless and widows in their affliction, and to keep himself unspotted from the world."

When was the last time you visited orphans and widows? When was the last time you comforted someone in affliction? Are you unspotted from the world? Do you watch R-rated and sexy movies? Do you listen to filthy music? Cheat on your taxes? Lie to your boss and co-workers?

You call yourself a Christian—the real deal—but do you do the good you know you should do? Look at James 4:17 (GW), "Whoever *knows* what is right but doesn't do it is *sinning*." And Romans 14:23 says, "…whatsoever *is* not of faith is *sin*."

Do you see how you can constantly be sinning and not asking God for forgiveness? What good thing do you KNOW you should be doing but are not? My brother, my sister, could you—could I—be "living in sin"?

To know what is good and right yet refuse to do it is open rebellion against God, which brings shame, guilt, and condemnation. Some of you may say, "I have faith in God and faith is simply 'hearing' the word." Really? Let's go there and compare scripture with scripture.

Romans 10:16 says, "So then faith cometh by *hearing*, and hearing by the word of God." Of course this is true. You must first hear and understand the Word of God in order to have and build faith. But it's deeper than this.

If *hearing* is all that needs to take place, why did Paul say of Israel "But I say, Have they not heard? Yes verily, their sound went into all the earth, and their words unto the ends of the world" (Romans 10:18). Isaiah also said about Israel, "All day long I have stretched out my hands to disobedient and rebellious people" (Romans 10:21 -GW).

Did you catch that? Did they not *hear* the teachings of God? By all means they did! Why then did he call them disobedient and rebellious? Because they failed to DO what the word required. By refusing to PRACTICE what was preached, their hearts became hardened (rebellious).

It was the same situation in Noah's day. Noah preached for many years (by his words and actions), warning the people about a flood to come. But only eight people were saved (Genesis 7:7, 13; Hebrews 11:7; 1 Peter 3:20; 2 Peter 2:5). *Eight* people! Did the rest of them not hear the warning? Of course they did. But they did not *heed* the warnings, and they perished for not acting on the truth they heard.

Here is a clearer exposition of Paul's understanding of this matter. Look at Romans 2:13: "For not the *hearers* of the law are just before God, but **the doers** of the law shall be justified (have God's approval)." Wow! How about that?

Let's continue in verses 14 and 15 of Romans 10, "For when the Gentiles without the law have a natural desire to do the things in the law, they are a law to themselves." (BBE) "They show that some requirements found in Moses' Teachings are written in their hearts. Their consciences speak to them. Their thoughts accuse them on one occasion and defend them on another." (GW)

Look closely at those words. It's not hearing *alone* that produces faith. It is *doing* what you hear and applying or living out what you believe that demonstrates true faith. Faith without action is **no faith at all.** Faith is belief in action. Faith is belief lived out. Faith *does* stuff.

Let's not just *read* or *hear* God's words. We need to **do** it. Live it. Practice it. Look at James 2:17-20 (GW), "… Faith by itself is dead if it doesn't cause you to **do** any good things. Another person might say, 'You have faith, but I do good things.' Show me your faith apart from the good things you do. I will show you my faith by the good things I do. You believe that there is one God. That's fine! The demons also believe that, and they tremble with fear. You fool! Do you have to be shown that faith which does nothing is *useless*?"

If you want to find a man or woman of faith, look for a man or woman of **action**, a man or woman **doing** what they believe and what they **know** to be the truth. Personally speaking, I would rather do the little I know faithfully than to faithfully learn a lot, but never put what I learn into action. Even businessman Jim Rohn said, "Learn, practice, and share your faith."

How about you? How do you answer the question, "Am I a Real Christian?" Is the Holy Spirit convicting you of your true standing before God? It is crucial to our eternal destiny to answer honestly. Be careful not to miss entering Canaan like that generation of Israel of old.

Many of them missed the Promised Land because "the word preached did not profit them, not being mixed with faith in them that **heard** it" (Hebrews 4:2). "Let us have a strong desire to come into that rest, and let no one go after the example of those who went against God's orders" (Hebrews 4:11- BBE).

The Israelites did not miss the promise land because they didn't hear or didn't know. They could not enter because of unbelief, disobedience, not doing right, and not living up to the light they had.

That's exactly how it will be at Jesus' second coming. Many will be lost, not because they didn't hear about it or didn't know, but because they refused to believe enough to act on what they heard and knew.

After all, Matthew 24:14 lets us know that the gospel will be preached in all the world for a witness. If that is true, then everyone will HEAR and everyone will KNOW. The problem is, Will everyone obey, do, apply, or practice what they hear and learn?

So, are you the real deal? Are you a REAL Christian? Let's look at some other scriptures. Revelation 1:3 says, "Blessed is he that *readeth*, and they that *hear* the words of this prophecy, and **keep** those things which are written therein: for the time is at hand."

Here we see that it's good to read and hear, but it's not complete until you **keep** or **DO** those things that are written. My friend, God is looking for people who are living examples of His teachings. Not just readers or hearers only.

How about Revelation 22:14? "Blessed are they that **do** his commandments, that they may have right to the tree of life, and may enter in through the gates into the city."

This verse is touchy. Many people have a problem with the Commandments of God, but how can a child of God hate the commands of God? This makes no sense. How is it that we can observe millions of man-made laws but frown upon God's Commandments?

Jesus was a doer of His Father's will. He kept His Father's commandments and we should follow His example (1 Peter 2:21). He said in John 14:31 (GW), "I want the world to know that I love the Father and that I am *doing* exactly what the Father has commanded me to do."

In John 15:10 (GW) He said, "If you obey my commandments, you will live in my love. I have *obeyed* my Father's commandments, and in that way I live in his love."

Ordering your life according to God's words (His commands or teachings) is a sign of love. If you're not doing what the Bible teaches then you're not walking in love towards God or Christ.

Jesus said in John 14:15, "If you love me, keep (*do, obey*) my commandments." How can you love God and not obey His principles?

John 14:21 (GW) declares, "Whoever **knows** and **obeys** my commandments is the person who loves me. Those who love me will have my Father's love, and I, too, will love them and show myself to them."

Christ said again in John 15:14, "You are my friends, if you do (obey) whatsoever I command you." Based on that text, are you a friend of God? Be honest with yourself. Do you keep God's commandments? Will the *real* Christian please stand up?

How about Matthew 12:50? Here, Jesus clearly states who His true family members are, "For whosoever shall **do** the will of my Father which is in heaven, the same is my brother, and sister, and mother."

This may seem a bit harsh, but too many preachers are preaching *feel-good* sermons. If you have cancer, you need to know it early. Jesus is longing to see His character reflected in us. It's time to get serious and right with God! You don't want to be caught off guard saying, "Lord, Lord…?" Use this time to get back on track.

Some people may say, "But Chance, the commandments have been 'done away' with."

Come on! Give me a break! Who are you kidding? You know that's not true, so stop deceiving yourself!

Read what Jesus said about this in Matthew 5:17-18, "Think not that I am come to destroy the law, or the prophets: I am not come to destroy, but to fulfill. For verily I say unto you, Till heaven and earth pass, one jot or one tittle shall in no wise pass from the law, till all be fulfilled." Clear enough?

Pay close attention to the next verse, "Whosoever therefore shall break one of these least commandments, and shall teach men so, he shall be called (named, considered) the *least* in the kingdom of heaven: but whosoever shall *do* and *teach* them, the same shall be called (named, considered) *great* in the kingdom of heaven" (Matthew 5:19).

Do you want to be called *least or unimportant* in heaven? I think you get the point. People compromise God's commandments because His laws cut into what they want. The principles of God are inconvenient to them.

Stop fooling yourself, saying and teaching that the laws of God don't matter. All God's Ten Commandments are important and apply today. Do you want anyone to kill you? Do you want someone to steal from you? Would you like someone to have an affair with your husband/wife? Do I hear you say No? Then I guess the Commandments are OK—right?

Now that we've settled that issue, turn to 1 John 3:22 which says, "And whatsoever we ask, we receive of him, (why?) *because* we keep his commandments, and *do* those things that are pleasing in his sight."

Let's hear now from the wisest man who ever lived (after Jesus, of course). King Solomon says in Ecclesiastes 12:13-14 (GW), "After having *heard* it all, this is the conclusion: *Fear God,* and *keep his commands*, because this applies to everyone (this is the whole duty of man). God will certainly judge everything that is done. This includes every secret thing, whether it is good or bad."

Note this life principle: *Doing is better than (just) knowing.* Knowing what to do is one thing but doing it is another. We're not saying that knowing is unimportant because you cannot *do* without first *knowing* what to do. To *be* more or *do* more, you must *know* more.

However, after we know what to do, we must actually *do it. Action* is the key word here. **Act on what you know.**

Knowing won't really get you anywhere, but *doing what you know* will get you everywhere.

In Matthew 23:1-4 (GW), Jesus said to the crowds and to his disciples, "The scribes and the Pharisees teach with Moses' authority. So be careful to do everything they tell you. But don't follow their example, because *they don't practice what they preach.* They make loads that are hard to carry and lay them on the shoulders of the people. However, they are not willing to lift a finger to move them."

For example, people don't just want to be told they are loved, they want to *experience* love. That takes some doing-- some deliberate action. Don't just say "I love you," show it. Show me how much you love me, don't just tell me. Let me know by your actions. Christ demonstrated His love for us, not only by *telling* us, but by *redeeming* us with His blood and life (Romans 5:8; John 3:16; 1 John 3:16, 18).

This was Jesus' instruction to His followers, "A new commandment I give unto you, That ye love one another as I have loved you, that ye also love one another. By this shall all men know that ye are my disciples, *if* ye have love one to another" (John 13:34-35). See also 1 John 2:7-8 and 2 John 1:5-6.

Do you have sincere love for people, even your enemies— though they be your brother, sister, spouse, or children? "He that saith he is in the light, and hateth his brother, is in darkness even until now. He that loveth his brother abideth in the light, and there is none occasion of stumbling in him. But he that hateth his brother is in darkness, and walketh in darkness, and knoweth not whither he goeth, because that darkness hath blinded his eyes" (1 John 2:9-11).

When you get down to the nitty-gritty of *real* Christianity, there's stuff we just don't like. Consider the command to forgive others. It is one of the most neglected spiritual disciplines, yet how often do we carry resentment? We're easily offended at times and withhold forgiveness, yet we want God to readily forgive us and to "remember our sins no more." How about you? When a brother or sister or family member injures you, do you easily grant forgiveness? The Golden Rule principle is easier said than done, isn't it?

How do you expect God to answer your prayers when you harbor an unforgiving spirit? Have you not read, "For if ye forgive men their trespasses, your heavenly Father will also forgive you: But if ye forgive not men their trespasses, neither will your Father forgive your trespasses" (Matthew 6:14-15)? How about, "Take heed to yourselves: If thy brother trespass against thee, rebuke him; and if he repent, forgive him. And if he trespass against thee seven times in a day, and seven times in a day turn again to thee, saying, I repent; thou shalt forgive him" (Luke 17:3-4)?

This self analysis goes deep, doesn't it? But even if it hurts, there's still hope. Don't miss reading the next few pages. For now, let the Word do its diagnosis so you'll know exactly what and where your spiritual illness is.

Read through the checklist in the following passage from Paul and honestly state if these maladies are still within you.

Put a check mark next to each one and ask again, "Am I a Real Christian?"

*"Wherefore putting away lying,*
*speak every man truth with his neighbour: for we are members one of another.*
*Be ye angry, and sin not: let not the sun go down upon your wrath:*
*Neither give place to the devil.*
*Let him that stole steal no more:*
*but rather let him labour, working with his hands the thing which is good,*
*that he may have to give to him that needeth.*
*Let no corrupt communication proceed out of your mouth, but that which is good to the use of edifying, that it may minister grace unto the hearers.*
*And grieve not the Holy Spirit of God, whereby ye are sealed unto the day of redemption.*
*Let all bitterness,*
*and wrath,*
*and anger,*
*and clamor (screaming, shouting, yelling),*
*and evil speaking, be put away from you,*
*with all malice (hatred, spite, meanness, cruelty)"*
(Ephesians 4:25-31).

Consider now three powerful illustrations in light of Jesus' second coming. What lessons can you learn from them?

**1. The Parable of the Sower: (Matthew 13:18-23 - GW)**
"Listen to what the story about the farmer means. Someone *hears* the word about the kingdom but doesn't understand

it. The evil one comes at once and snatches away what was planted in him. This is what the seed planted along the road illustrates. The seed planted on rocky ground is the person who *hears* the word and accepts it at once with joy. Since he doesn't have any root, he lasts only a little while. When suffering or persecution comes along because of the word, he immediately falls from faith. The seed planted among thorn bushes is another person who *hears the word*. But the worries of life and the deceitful pleasures of riches choke the word so that it can't produce anything. But the seed planted on good ground is the person who *hears and understands the word*. This type produces crops. They produce one hundred, sixty, or thirty times as much as was planted."

Notice that all three classes heard the word, but only one produced. All *knew* the Word but *only* one *"did"* the word and got results. Which class of hearers are you? What other principles can you unearth from this parable?

**2. The Wise and Foolish Men (Matthew 7:24-27)**
"… Whosoever heareth these sayings of mine, and *doeth* them, I will liken him unto a wise man, which built his house upon a rock: And the rain descended, and the floods came, and the winds blew, and beat upon that house; and it fell not: for it was founded upon a rock. And every one that heareth these sayings of mine, and *doeth them not,* shall be likened unto a foolish man, which built his house upon the sand: And the rain descended, and the floods came, and the winds blew, and beat upon that house; and it fell: and great was the fall of it."

What was the difference between the wise and the fool? One word... *Doing!* Both heard the word but only the wise did what the word commanded.

Who are the wise again according to Matthew 7:24? The wise are those who hear and **do** the will of God. Conversely, the foolish are those who hear, but do **not** do.

Are you a fool? You may be quick to answer "No," but the Bible says you ARE a fool *if* you hear only, but don't do. I pray you'll make the decision to be wise instead of foolish.

**3. The Wise and Foolish Virgins. (Matthew 25:1-13)**
Right after giving the long list of the signs of the times in Matthew 24, Jesus gives this striking parable. The virgins here are all Christians. They represent the dichotomy of professed believers—**wise** (obedient/doers of the word) and **foolish** (disobedient/hearers only).

They all knew the bridegroom was coming but all did not adequately prepare themselves to meet Him. The foolish virgins forfeited their right to the marriage simply because they refused to take oil with them. How can you keep your lamp burning without oil?

At the time of Jesus' coming, some will be ready and some will not. What sets them apart is that only a few will choose to believe and act upon the words of God concerning the coming crisis and the imminent return of Christ.

Chew on these quotations from one of my favorite authors. "The greatest deception of the human mind in Christ's day was that a mere assent to the truth constitutes righteousness. In all human experience a theoretical knowledge of the truth has been proved to be *insufficient* for the saving of the soul. It does not bring forth the fruits of righteousness. . . . The Pharisees *claimed* to be children of Abraham, and boasted of their possession of the oracles of God; yet these advantages did **not** preserve them from selfishness, malignity, greed for gain, and the basest hypocrisy. . ." (*The Faith I Live By,* p. 108).

"The same danger still exists. Many take it for granted that they are Christians, simply because they subscribe to certain theological tenets. But *they have not brought the truth into practical life.* They have not believed and loved it, therefore they have not received the power and grace that come through sanctification of the truth. Men may profess faith in the truth; but *if it does not make them sincere, kind, patient, forbearing, heavenly-minded,* it is a **curse** to its possessors, and through their influence it is a curse to the world" (*The Desire of Ages,* p. 309).

In conclusion, I hope you had a good glimpse of where you are spiritually and your fitness for heaven. You can't separate who you are from what you do. You will be rewarded based on your deeds or actions. What you do speak louder than what you say. But you can't separate your words from your works either.

Jesus rebuked the Pharisees in Matthew 12:34-37 saying, "O generation of vipers, how can ye, being evil, speak good things? for *out of the abundance of the heart* the mouth speaketh. A good man out of the good treasure of the heart bringeth forth good things: and an evil man out of the evil treasure bringeth forth evil things. But I say unto you, That every idle word that men shall speak, they shall give account thereof in the day of judgment. For by thy words thou shalt be justified, and by thy words thou shalt be condemned."

Based on this, are you ready for judgment and heaven? Are your words and works in harmony? You will not be saved by your works, but because you are saved, will you not be doing or producing good works?

Are you giving glory to God by the way you live? At home? At work? At school or where ever you represent Christ? It's time to get serious. Will the *real* Christian please stand up?

"God has made us what we are. He has created us in Christ Jesus to live lives *filled with good works* that he has prepared for us to do" (Ephesians 2:10, GW).

"Let your light so shine before men, that they may see your good works and glorify your Father which is in heaven" (Matthew 5:16).

Christ needs true soldiers to stand on His side and lift up the standard of Truth in the land. Today, we are seeking a spiritual check-up. With all honesty, let us ask ourselves how we are spiritually. Don't try to fool yourself, but be brutally honest.

The Lord is saying, "Listen, you deaf people. Look, you blind people, so that you can see. Who is blind except my servant or deaf like the messenger I send? Who is blind like the one who has my trust or blind like the servant of the Lord? You have seen much, but you do not observe anything. Your ears are open, but you hear nothing. The Lord is pleased because he does what is right. He praises the greatness of his teachings and makes them glorious" (Isaiah 42:18-21 - GW).

If Jesus came today, how would you want Him to find you? What would be your reward? Would you be happy to see Jesus or would you be filled with regrets? The ball is in your court. *Will the real Christian please stand up?*

> "Watch therefore, for ye know neither the day nor the hour wherein the Son of man cometh" (Matthew 25:13).

# THE ROOT PROBLEM OF JUST *"KNOWING"*

As a reminder, we're studying the dichotomy within Christianity—between those who are true Christians and those who only *profess* to be Christians.

In the last chapter, "Will the REAL Christian please stand up?" we discovered the difference between *knowing* and *doing* and what it really means to *BE* a Christian.

That is a hard message because it challenges us to make an honest assessment of where we really are on this Christian journey.

Are you part of the group that embodies the life of Christ by your thoughts, words, and actions? Or are you a Christian who only "professes" to know God, while your actions betray you?

Are you *really* a Christian? Have you examined yourself to see whether you are still in the faith? Did you pass the spiritual check up?

In the next chapter, "CURES for Mediocre Christianity", we'll discuss Biblical solutions to overcoming the dichotomy between being a Real Christian and a Professing Christian. You'll learn how to not just *know* what is good for you, but even more important, how to *DO* the good you know, and when you ought to do it.

This chapter is called, "The ROOT Problem of Just *'Knowing'*." As you read, you'll uncover the reason behind the problem. You'll understand WHY most Christians live on the low-to-average plains of life.

Christ said in Matthew 7:21 (GW), "Not everyone who says to me, 'Lord, Lord!' will enter the kingdom of heaven, but **only the person who does** what my Father in heaven wants." He also said in Luke 6:46 (BBE), "Why do you say to me, Lord, Lord, and **do not** the things which I say (teach)?"

My friend, knowing what you should do is one thing. Knowing *how* to do it and actually *doing* it are different matters altogether. We live in a world today of many KNOWERS but few DOERS. There's much learning, but little practical application of knowledge learned. This mentality has crept into God's church—so much so that you can't tell who's a real Christian and who's not.

Scripture does not promote hearing without doing. James 1:22 says, "But be ye doers of the word, and not hearers only, deceiving your own selves." James 4:17 says, "Therefore to him that knoweth to do good, and doeth it not, to him it is sin."

There's no getting around obedience to God's laws and instructions. "A theoretical knowledge of the truth is essential, but the knowledge of the greatest truth *will not save us;* our knowledge must be practical. God's people must not only know His will, but they **must practice it.** Many will be purged out from the numbers of those who know the truth, because they are not sanctified by it. The truth must be brought into their hearts, sanctifying and cleansing them from all earthliness and sensuality in the most private life. The soul temple must be cleansed. Every secret act is as if we were in the presence of God and holy angels, as all things are open before God, and from Him nothing can be hid" (*Testimonies on Sexual Behavior, Adultery, and Divorce,* p. 86).

If the truth you subscribe to does not change you, sanctify, and purify you, you may be purged out of the number of true saints going to heaven. Yes, it's that serious.

The time is now when we must be harmonious in our belief, words, and actions. The time has come for us to move from a mere theological assent to truth to a consistent daily application of those truths. Jesus said to His followers in Matthew 5:20, "… except your righteousness shall exceed the righteousness of the scribes and Pharisees, *ye shall in no case enter into the kingdom* of heaven."

I suppose by now you may be questioning and reasoning, "I know all these things and I truly desire to live the way Christ wants me to, but I cannot! I want to do the good I know to do but I keep doing what I don't want to do and I keep falling back into sin! How can I DO the things of Christ on a regular and consistent basis?"

Before we get to the HOW, which is covered in the next chapter, you must understand the WHY behind your reluctance to do the good you know you need to do. You must get to the ROOT problem of just *"Knowing"* which is causing you to live on the low-to-average plain of Christianity.

This hypocrisy between real and professing Christians is best understood in Romans 7:14-24. This passage is the key to the WHY problem of KNOWERS vs. DOERS. Today we're going to dissect it verse by verse. Try underlining or taking notes. This chapter contains vital and key concepts.

Romans 7:14 (GW): "I know that God's standards (laws) are spiritual, but I have a corrupt (carnal) nature, sold as a slave to sin." Here is the reason for duplicity among Christians. The problem is not with God or His laws (commandments).

Romans 7:12 says, "Wherefore the law is holy, and the commandment holy, and just, and good." So why do people say God's laws or commandments are not good and we don't have to keep them? It doesn't make sense! How could something holy, just, and good be condemned as the exact opposite?

God's laws and commands are a transcript of His character. Like God, His laws and commands are holy, just, and good. So the problem is not with God and His teachings. Where then does the problem lie? What is the root or source of disobedience?

Romans 7:14 positively identifies the root of the problem— The problem is with SELF! With YOU! Yes. **You** are your own problem! The carnal, corrupt, evil, deceitful flesh of yours is the real reason why you don't do what you know you need to do. And yes, I am a problem also.

King David said in Psalm 51:5, "Behold, I was shapen in iniquity; and in sin did my mother conceive me." Even from birth we have problems with sin!

## The Root Problem of Just *"Knowing"*

For example, parents don't need to teach children to lie. Children automatically lie—and at a very early age! They deceive their parents by crying when they want attention, but the parents think the child is hungry or something is wrong. So sin is a problem we are born with, and we cannot get rid of it except God intervenes.

Therefore, the *struggle is with the sin nature*—you're enslaved to sin and bad habits. Our flesh is constantly at war with anything holy, just, and good. The commands and teachings of God are the good we know we should follow, but the carnal flesh is like a slave master—it keeps us in bondage to what we don't like.

Verse 15: "I don't realize what I'm doing. *I don't do what I want to do.* Instead, **I do what I hate**." There it is! Everyone has this struggle. This is why you procrastinate, why you disobey the good commands of God, and why you live like the world, all the while claiming to be a Christian.

You need to understand your habits, patterns, and struggles. You don't do the good and right things you need to do. Instead, you do the exact opposite. You know what to do but you don't do it!

Look at verse 16: "I don't do what I want to do, but I agree that God's standards are good." Here Paul is saying that since he's unable to do the good and right things of the Law, since in his flesh he does not carry out the teachings of God, he consents to the Law (God's Word) that it is good indeed. This defeats the erroneous teaching that God's Commandments are not valid today. It also shows the power of the Law of

God. You and I cannot (by our own will power) measure up to its holy and just standards. That's why we need Christ.

Even though that may be the case, Romans 7:7 says, "What shall we say then? Is the law sin? God forbid. Nay, I had not known sin, but by the law: for I had not known lust, except the law had said, Thou shalt not covet."

Again, the problem is not the law. The problem is not God. There is no occasion here to blame God or anyone else for your spiritual malady. You cannot blame anyone, because the problem does not lie outside you. In fact, the problem is YOU! Stop making excuses and start looking into the mirror of God's Law, and He'll show you and lead you to the solution to your problem.

James 1:23-25 teaches, "For if any be a hearer of the word, and not a doer, he is like unto a man beholding his natural face in a glass: For he beholdeth himself, and goeth his way, and straightway forgetteth what manner of man he was. But whoso looketh into the perfect law of liberty, and *continueth* therein, he being not a forgetful hearer, but a **doer** of the work, this man shall be blessed in his deed."

The Law of God is like a mirror. It points out what's wrong in your life but it does not correct the problem. When you look into a mirror and see dirt or lint, does the mirror remove the dirt or lint? No. The mirror serves a good purpose in showing you that you don't look as good as you think.

Imagine you go to work one day looking and feeling good because you're wearing a new suit that looks very nice. The morning rolls on as usual, with meetings and co-worker interactions. Everyone compliments you on the nice suit, which boosts your self-confidence even more. Now imagine the shock you feel at noon when you go to the bathroom and glance in the mirror. Horrors! All morning you've had a good-sized booger hanging out your nose, with crust still in the side of your eye!

Your self-confidence now sinks to utter humiliation because you were walking around all day confident that you looked good. Remember all the people you spoke with around 9:00 am. They saw how you really were! They saw the booger and crust but you *acted* like everything was fine. Your boss and manager had a totally different picture of you all morning. They saw past the nice suit and couldn't help but wonder if you had looked into the mirror before leaving the house.

Here's a question: Can you blame the mirror for not pointing out the booger and crust? Wouldn't you have been happier if you had gone to the mirror sooner to discover your faults? Then you would not have suffered embarrassment because you would have fixed the problem before going to work. You may have even said something like, "Thank God I checked the mirror this morning." Or, "Praise God I saw my face before leaving the house!"

This is exactly how God's Law functions in your life. It shows your errors and points to what and *Who* is good. But the Law itself doesn't change what's wrong.

Verse 17, "So I am no longer the one who is doing the things I hate, but *sin that lives in me is doing them.*" Paul is not passing blame or whining that he can't do the good things he desires. He's letting you know that SIN is the reason why you do the things you hate and don't do the right things you know you should do.

But don't despair. We're all in the same boat. "For all have sinned, and come short of the glory of God" (Romans 3:23). Do you see how powerful sin is and why you can't dwell in the flesh? *You must daily crucify the sinful nature.*

The truth of the matter is, *your sinful nature is at war with God's standards.* The reason why you don't live and act like a Christian on a daily basis is because sin is still reigning in your mortal body. This should not be the case with God's children.

Paul admonished in Romans 6:12-16, "Let not sin therefore reign in your mortal body, that ye should obey it in the lusts thereof. Neither yield ye your members as instruments of unrighteousness unto sin: but *yield yourselves unto God,* as those that are alive from the dead, and your members *as* instruments of righteousness unto God. For *sin shall not have dominion over you:* for ye are not under the law, but under grace. What then? shall we sin, because we are not under the law, but under grace? *God forbid.* Know ye not, that to whom ye yield yourselves servants to obey, **his servants ye are to whom ye obey**; *whether of sin unto death, or of obedience unto righteousness?*"

If you find that you're not living up to God's ideal, then you're still a servant of sin which leads to death. The choice is yours. Paul says we should yield ourselves to God, not to sin and unrighteousness. Because we're under God's grace, the power of sin over us is broken. Sin should not be controlling you. Stop serving and yielding to sin. Serve God! Surrender to the Holy Spirit.

## The Root Problem of Just *"Knowing"*

We're now at Romans 7:18, which tells me that nothing good lives in me; that is, nothing good lives in my corrupt nature. Although I have the desire to do what is right, I don't do it.

What a powerful thought! How can the Apostle Paul make it any clearer? The *root problem* for living on the low-to-average plains of life is *sin*. In your sinful flesh, there is nothing good. Let me say that again. *In your sinful flesh, there is **nothing good**.* No matter how much you *TRY* to live up to God's principles, you CANNOT do it in the sinful nature.

The sinful flesh *cannot* be saved or redeemed. Your sin nature must **die**. It must be crucified and every evil tendency must die with it. Though you have the mind and will to do right, to obey, and to live as a Christian, you don't have the power and ability in the flesh to perform the good you know you should do.

Say to yourself, "Without Christ, I am sinful and nothing good will ever come out of my sinful flesh. I can't even do what is right." Brothers and sisters, you *cannot* please God by living in your flesh, "Because the carnal mind is enmity against God: for *it is not subject to the law of God*, **neither indeed can be.** So then they that are in the flesh **cannot please God**" (Romans 8:7-8).

Some of us pretend we serve God when in fact we serve our sinful desires. These verses make it abundantly clear that our corrupt natures cannot please God. The carnal mind will not subject itself to God's authority. It won't even *try* to do so. Your corrupt flesh will never yield control to the instructions of God. Therefore, it must die! Not slowly, but immediately and daily. Starve it. Defeat it. Kill it!

I hope you're getting an accurate view of the striking dichotomy within Christianity. That's why Jesus was straightforward in saying, "Not everyone that saith unto me, Lord, Lord, shall enter into the kingdom of heaven; but he that doeth the will of my Father which is in heaven" (Matthew 7:21).

Plain and straight, those who don't carry out God's teachings are none of His. Why? Because they are servants of the flesh and not servants of the Spirit. Those who are in Christ live according to the Spirit and are free from condemnation (Romans 8:1). God's Spirit makes us His children and that's the difference between a mere professing Christian and a Real Christian. Are you a REAL Christian?

If you are averse to God's laws and standards, then it may be that you are certainly still in the flesh—a mere *professing* Christian. "For they that are after the flesh do mind the things of the flesh; but they that are after the Spirit the things of the Spirit. For to be carnally minded *is* death; but to be spiritually minded *is* life and peace" (Romans 8:5-6).

Let's continue with our main passage. Romans 7:19, "*I don't do the good I want to do.* Instead, **I do the evil that I don't want to do.**" This verse depicts the great controversy between good and evil like none other. It's why you do what you hate even though you know better. That's the problem we all find ourselves in. It's not a problem of knowing, but a problem of doing—a problem of obedience.

You desire to do good things like being on time, getting important tasks accomplished, speaking kindly to your children and spouse, using your time wisely and productively, keeping your eyes and mind single to God's glory, and having regular and consistent devotional time with Jesus.

However, the evil you don't want to do, that's what you end up doing. You may even lie or cheat. You get to work or church late, then make lame excuses. You procrastinate about getting your job or homework done. You become angry and perhaps even abusive with your children or spouse. You waste countless hours browsing the Internet and Facebook. You privately watch R-rated movies and pornography. But once in a while you manage to squeeze in ten minutes for prayer and Bible study! What a horrible way to live! No wonder you remain on the average–to-low plains of life.

On to verse 20 of Romans 7, "Now, when I do what I don't want to do, I am no longer the one who is doing it. **Sin that lives in me is doing it**." Again, sin is the culprit of your quagmire. Sin causes you to do those things you don't want to do and hinders you from doing the good you ought to do.

Verse 21, "So I've discovered this truth: Evil is present with me even when I want to do what God's standards say is good." Here is a life principle. "When you want to do good or what is right, you inevitably do wrong (the opposite) because evil is also present with you."

Verses 22-23, "I take pleasure in God's standards in my inner being. However, I see a different standard at work throughout my body. It is at war with the standards (law) my mind sets and tries to take me captive to sin's standards which still exist throughout my body."

From these verses we learn that although we know what is right and what God law requires, there's another law at war within us. This power enslaves us to do wrong, to procrastinate, to lie, cheat, and steal. The enemy constantly seeks to make us captive to the law of sin. Do not fall for his tricks!

Galatians 5:17, 19-21 (GW) depicts this inner battle. "What your corrupt nature wants is contrary to what your spiritual nature wants, and what your spiritual nature wants is contrary to what your corrupt nature wants. *They are opposed to each other.* As a result, you don't always do what you intend to do…Now, the effects of the corrupt nature are obvious: illicit sex, perversion, promiscuity, idolatry, drug use, hatred, rivalry, jealousy, angry outbursts, selfish ambition, conflict, factions, envy, drunkenness, wild partying, and similar things. I've told you in the past and I'm telling you again that **people who do these kinds of things will not inherit the kingdom of God.**"

I like how the apostle Paul makes everything clear. The Spirit and the flesh cannot occupy the same body at the same time and maintain peace. One will win over the other, and we determine daily which one wins the battle. Your mind wants to obey God's instructions, but your sinful nature is a slave to sin, causing you to live on the average-to-low plains of life. These two powers—the powers of good and evil are always raging war in your mind and body.

In this second chapter, you have positively identified *The Root of the Problem of Just "Knowing"* to be SIN—your sinful nature, the flesh, your carnal mind. You did not have to look too far did you? All you had to do was look into the mirror. The problem for your spiritual malady is you. Sin dwelling in you and sin controlling you.

If we remain in this condition of continually fulfilling the desires of our flesh, Paul reminds us that "people who do these kinds of things *will not* inherit the Kingdom of God." So we don't want to remain simply *professing* Christians, do we? We want to be *real* Christians who stand up for Christ!

So how can we remedy the problem?

We begin by recognizing our spiritual state and crying out like the Apostle Paul in Romans 7:24, "O wretched man that I am! Who shall deliver me from the body of this death?"

Perhaps you feel Paul's misery and pain. You are tired of *playing* Christian, tired of professing to be saved, and tired of your actions betraying you. Maybe you're asking yourself, "Am I a Real Christian?"

Then cry out like Paul, "Who shall deliver me from this pitiful existence?" Hope is on the way. "I thank God through Jesus Christ our Lord," he adds in the next verse. God hears our earnest pleas for help.

In the next chapter, **"CURES for Mediocre Christianity,"** we'll explore how to overcome the hypocrisy between being a real Christian and a professing Christian only. We'll learn how to not just *know* what is good for us, but more importantly, how to *do* the good we know, and *when* we ought to do it.

Thank God for revealing in His Word insights as to why we've been unable to do what we need to do. The next chapter will reveal the power of God to transform our lives and move us from mediocre Christianity to victorious living.

> "For when we were in the flesh, the motions of sins, which were by the law, did work in our members to bring forth fruit unto death. But now we are delivered from the law, that being dead wherein we were held; that we should serve in newness of spirit, and not in the oldness of the letter." (Romans 7:5-6)

# CURES FOR MEDIOCRE CHRISTIANITY

"*Am I a Real Christian?*" is an important question you should ask yourself. This book provides a spiritual check-up for Christians. Consider it a diagnostic test to help determine if you're ready for the imminent return of our wonderful Savior who loves us so.

So far we've studied the difference between Knowing and Doing, and what it really means to BE a Christian. In the chapter, *"Will the Real Christian Please Stand up?"* we made an honest assessment of where we *really* are on this Christian journey. That message may have been a wakeup call, helping us understand from the mouth of Jesus and His apostles that being a Christian is more than simply believing or having knowledge about God. True Christians not only *hear* God's words, they live them out daily.

In the last chapter, *The Root Problem of Just "Knowing,"* perhaps you gained insights into WHY many Christians live on the low-to-average plains of life. SIN is the root problem behind our reluctance to do the good we know we need to do.

We also studied the war taking place within us—a war between our spiritual and carnal natures. The corrupt, sinful flesh cannot please God. It refuses to submit to God's holy, just, and good standards. Therefore, we're tugged in two directions. On one hand, we desire to serve and obey God, but on the other hand, sin present in us urges us to do the bad things we hate and not the good things we know.

We then grappled with Paul's theological exposition of this dilemma in Romans 7:18-23 (GW). He explains, "I know that **nothing** good lives in me; that is, nothing good lives in my corrupt nature. Although I have the desire to do what is right, I don't do it. I don't do the good I want to do. Instead, I do the evil that I don't want to do. Now, when I do what I don't want to do, I am no longer the one who is doing it. *Sin that lives in me is doing it.* So I've discovered this truth: *Evil is present with me even when I want to do what God's standards say is good.* I take pleasure in God's standards in my inner being. However, I see a different standard at work throughout my body. It is at war with the standards my mind sets and tries to take me captive to sin's standards which still exist throughout my body."

Could anyone have made this teaching any clearer? It's the perfect explanation of sin's power to enslave and attempt to keep us out of the Kingdom of God.

However, it's not enough to know sin is the reason why we live as hypocrites, professing to be real Christians but sometimes living like devils at home. It doesn't change the fact that Jesus says, "Not everyone that saith unto me, Lord, Lord, shall enter into the kingdom of heaven; but he that doeth the will of my Father which is in heaven" (Matthew 7:21). Or, "Why call ye me, Lord, Lord, and do not the things which I say?" (Luke 6:46)

We can't blame sin or the flesh and give up in despair. Like Paul, we must cry out, "Oh wretched man that I am! Who shall deliver (rescue) me from the body of this death?" (Romans 7:24)

If that is truly your cry today, then God has heard your prayer for help. You can say with David in Psalm 6:9, "The Lord hath heard my supplication; the Lord will receive my prayer."

In this last part of our study, we are about to find God's powerful solutions to overcome mediocre Christianity. You will no longer have to be a *Knower* (or *Hearer*) only, but a *Doer* of the Word. It's time to live like the champions God made us to be and discover the power available to every child of God through Him.

Today, you will discover the remedy for living on the low-to-average plains of life. You'll find the prescription for your spiritual malady. After undergoing this spiritual check-up that Paul advises, let's now begin to enjoy restored spiritual health.

In 2 Corinthians 13:5-8 (GW), we read, "**Examine** yourselves to see whether you are still in the (Christian) faith. Test (prove) yourselves! Don't you recognize that you are people in whom Jesus Christ lives? Could it be that you're failing the test? I hope that you will realize that we haven't failed the test. We pray to God that you won't do anything wrong. It's not that we want to prove that we've passed the test. Rather, we want you to do whatever is right, even if we seem to have failed. We can't do anything against the truth but only to help the truth."

We are living in a time when conformity to secularism, humanism, and skepticism is the norm. Sadly, many so-called Christians subscribe to these ideologies, but we must change, and we must change *now*! This is not a time for compromise and conformity (Romans 12:2). Now is the time for *revival, reformation, and transformation*. "Now *it is* high time to **awake out of sleep:** for now *is* our salvation nearer than when we believed. The night is far spent, the day is at hand: let us therefore cast off the works of darkness, and let us put on the armour of light. Let us walk honestly, as in the day; not in rioting and drunkenness, not in chambering and wantonness, not in strife and envying" (Romans 13:11-13).

If we continue to deliberately live in sin—in open rebellion to the known teachings of God, we will miss out on eternal life. "For the wages of sin *is* death… Sin, when it is finished, bringeth forth death" (Romans 6:23a; James 1:15b).

We're not talking about the occasional mistakes you and I make as Christians, we're talking about living in continuous sin. If doing wrong, going against God's will, is not appalling to your spiritual nature, then something is wrong. That is the problem we are pleading with God to correct in us. This is a message of hope and not of condemnation. It's a balm to heal the wounded soul. Christ is coming! Delay not one day longer in preparation.

The following **Seven Cures for Mediocre Christianity** will revive the fire we had when we first accepted Christ. If you don't know Christ yet, then these Seven Cures will help you find Him. These are the solutions you've been waiting for, and today, by God's power, let's kick sin and Satan to the "pit of hell" where they belong.

> "... Give diligence to make your calling and election sure: for if ye do these things, ye shall never fall"
> (2 Peter 1:10).

## CURE # 1: Remember Who You Are and Whose You Are.

Sometimes people forget their true identity, so they live a double life. They live like someone they're not, and this confuses others. Can you imagine Microsoft's billionaire, Bill Gates' son living like a pauper, eating out of the trash and sleeping on the streets? Would you not think he was either crazy or just plain dumb?

Well, that is how we are as Christians. We live defeated, discouraged, and dull lives. No wonder people can't tell whether or not we are the real deal! Stop living like an imposter.

God purchased your life and freedom with His own blood (Acts 20:28; Ephesians 1:14; Mark 10:45). Therefore, you don't need to be addicted to sinful pleasures. You don't need to wallow in the miasma of continuous disobedience. You are a child of God. You are FREE.

"If the Son therefore shall make you free, ye shall be **free indeed.**" "Stand fast therefore in the liberty wherewith Christ hath made us free, and *be not entangled again* with the yoke of bondage" (John 8:36; Galatians 5:1).

My brothers and sisters, what are you doing with the power God gave you? Have you traded your birthright for a mess of porridge like Esau (Hebrews 12:16)? Have you not read, "But as many as received him, to them gave he **power** to become the sons of God, *even* to them that believe on his name: Which were born, not of blood, *nor of the will of the flesh,* nor of the will of man, *but of God?*" (John 1:12-13)

Hallelujah! What a heritage for the child of God. You have power! The gates of hell cannot prevail against you (Matthew 16:18). "No weapon that is formed against thee shall prosper; and every tongue *that* shall rise against thee in judgment thou shalt condemn. This *is* the heritage of the servants of the Lord, and their righteousness *is* of me, saith the Lord" (Isaiah 54:17).

My friend, your righteousness is from your Father in heaven. His image is being reproduced in you. Have no fear of falling and let not the enemy taunt you with accusations of how filthy you are.

You are born again, not of the flesh, but of God. "Therefore if any man *be* in Christ, *he is* a **new creature**: old things are passed away; behold, **all things** are become new" (2 Corinthians 5:17).

How many things are become new for the child of God? Not some things, or most things, but *all* things! That means you are no longer in bondage to the flesh. That means the old nature has died and you are now spiritual. "That which is born of the flesh is flesh; and that which is born of the Spirit is spirit" (John 3:6). "They which are the children of the flesh, these are not the children of God: but the children of the promise are counted for the seed" (Romans 9:8).

Listen, God is your Daddy! You are His child and because you put your faith, hope, and trust in Him, He will perfect that which concerns you (Psalm 138:8). He is the author and finisher of your faith (Hebrews 12:2a). Be confident that your heavenly Father will continue to complete the good work He started in you until Christ returns (Philippians 1:6). Accept, believe, and claim this *by faith*. Remember *who* you are and *Whose* you are.

Because nothing is impossible for your Father, then nothing is impossible for you (Matthew 19:26; 17:20). This means that "sin shall not have dominion over you: for ye are not under the law, but under (God's) grace" (Romans 6:14). We have a divine mandate to be like our Father in all things and not be a slave to sinful habits. We should have dominion over our flesh and sin.

Paul says, "God be thanked, that ye *were* the servants of sin, but ye have obeyed from the heart that form of doctrine which was delivered you. Being then made free from sin, ye became the servants of righteousness" (Romans 6:17-18). Since you became righteous, you should be *doing* righteous things, not sinful things. "If ye know that he is righteous, ye know that *every one that doeth righteousness is born of him*" (1 John 2:29).

First John chapter 3 contains a very strong passage, so pay close attention. It is pivotal to our spiritual growth and wellbeing. A true indication of whether or not we are children of God is what we *do*. First John 3:7 says, "Little children, let no man deceive you: **he that doeth righteousness is righteous**, even as he is righteous."

Please don't miss this point. If you are continuously living in sin, hearing but not *doing* the words of God, then you have a serious spiritual disease. You have the cancer of a sinful nature still dwelling in you. Chances are, you have forgotten your birthright. You have turned your back on your heavenly Father and rekindled your passions with your other father, the devil.

If we deliberately continue to sin, which includes neglecting to live up the light we've been given, have we really become acquainted with Christ? The Bible says, "You are like your old father, the devil, because he has been sinning since the beginning." *Christ came to destroy the works of the devil,* and that means the vicious clutch of sin will be broken in our lives.

Continuing in 1 John 3:9-10 (TCW) we read, "No one who has been born of God will continue living a sinful life because the seed (nature) of God is within him, and he's been born again by the power of the Holy Spirit. This is the basic difference between the children of God and the children of the devil. Those who don't **do** what is right and don't *love their brothers and sisters* in Christ don't really belong to God."

Mercy! Help us, Lord! So, are you really a Christian? Fellow saint, the Bible is our standard. You and I cannot make up our own standards for what's right and what's wrong. The Bible clearly teaches the difference. Some of us seem to love everyone else, but we can't love the brother or sister across the aisle. We say we love the people in the world, but we sometimes don't even love our loved ones! Something is wrong when a Christian cannot love his wife or her husband. Something is wrong when you're still a racist. Something is desperately wrong when you can't love with pitying tenderness your fellow brothers and sisters at church.

"He that loveth not knoweth not God; for God is love. If a man say, I love God, and hateth his brother, he is a liar: for he that loveth not his brother whom he hath seen, how can he love God whom he hath not seen? And this commandment have we from him, That he who loveth God love his brother also" (1 John 4:8; 20-21).

This passage is extremely clear; the problem is you don't really love God. You don't *know* God—your loving, kind heavenly Father. Have you asked yourself, "Based on the principles I know directly from the Bible, Am I a Real Christian?"

If you're going to rise above this mediocrity and hypocrisy, you have to remember *who* you are and *Whose* you are, "for love is of God; and every one that loveth is born of God, and knoweth God" (1 John 4:7).

When you are a true child of God, you will think, speak, and act like your Father. If you don't, then you are a child of that other father. "For when ye were the servants of sin, ye were free from righteousness. But now being made free from sin, and become servants to God, ye have your fruit unto holiness, and the end everlasting life" (Romans 6:20-22). What kind of fruits are you bearing?

Get out of the dumpster! Stop drinking and eating the scraps of sin. Exercise your freedom in Christ. Take the power you've been given as a son or daughter of the Most High and exercise dominion over sin in your life.

If a slave refuses to be free, would you blame his master for keeping him in bondage? That's like when the Emancipation Act was signed, many slaves still returned to the same menial and degrading lifestyles under their slave masters.

The Emancipation Proclamation did not benefit them, not because it was faulty, but because they refused to be free. Some did not know they were free, some did not care that they were free, some did not want to be free, and some just did not know *how* to be free. The most pitiful of them all were those so entrenched in the mindset of a slave that all they could do was think and act like slaves even though they *knew* they were free.

Which one of these are you? Don't refuse to live like free men and women and thus make Christ's Emancipation Act in vain. Be like the class of freed slaves who, as soon as they *knew* they were free, left *everything* associated with slavery. They claimed their freedom by walking away. This act of walking away and moving as far away as possible from any semblance of slavery is the hallmark of a freed man or woman.

Today I say to you, "Take Cure #1 for mediocre Christianity— *Remember who you are and Whose you are.*" As a child of the King, you are royalty, you have eternal riches, you have a mansion on high, you have access to help from angels and power from the Holy Spirit. More than this, you have freedom and power in Christ, so "Stand fast therefore in the liberty wherewith Christ hath made us free, and be not entangled again with the yoke of bondage" (Galatians 5:1).

## CURE # 2: Depend on Christ and the Holy Spirit

If you look back at our passage in Romans 7:14-24, it ends with the Apostle Paul crying out, as many of us are, "O wretched man that I am! Who shall set me free from this sinful nature which is destined to die?" (Romans 7:24).

Praise God for what follows next—the second prescription for mediocre Christianity. Thank God, **Jesus Christ** is the antidote. He delivers us from the lethal nature of sinful flesh (Romans 7: 25a). The answer to living in obedience to the principles of God is through His Son. Like Jesus, depend upon God and the Holy Spirit to accomplish God's will in your life.

Obedience apart from Christ is impossible. That's why Israel of old could not measure up to the laws of God. Jesus said, "The Son can do nothing of himself, but what he seeth the Father do: for what things soever he doeth, these also doeth the Son likewise" (John 5:19). "I can of mine own self do nothing: as I hear, I judge: and my judgment is just; because I seek not mine own will, but the will of the Father which hath sent me" (John 5:30). "I *do nothing of myself;* but as my Father hath taught me, I speak these things. "…I do always those things that please him" (John 8:28-29).

If Christ could do nothing of Himself, what about you and me? If Christ depended on His Father and the Spirit, then how much more do we need to depend upon Him? If you've been going at it alone, it's no wonder you're in a spiritual quagmire. Who do you think you are to do it alone when your Savior said, "Without me you can do nothing?" (John 15:5)

How then do you turn around your spiritual dry season? You do it by Christ and His Spirit alone. The only way to please God is by faith (Hebrews 11:6). Faith in Christ and faith in God's power to save *from* sin unto righteousness. **You cannot do it on your own.** "For it is God which worketh in you both to will and to do of *his* good pleasure" (Philippians 2:13).

Christ is your hope of salvation. He is your redeemer. He is your strength. He is your victory. He is your righteousness. Jesus Christ is the King of Kings, and Lord of Lords! He is, "able to keep you from falling, and to present you faultless before the presence of his glory with exceeding joy" (Jude 1:24).

You may feel weak and insufficient right now, especially from the challenge of the first two chapters. You know Christ does not want you to sin, "My little children, these things write I unto you, that ye sin not" but, "if any man sin, we have an advocate with the Father, Jesus Christ the righteous: And he is the propitiation (atoning sacrifice) for our sins: and not for ours only, but also for the sins of the whole world" (1 John 2:1-2).

Praise God for that word! Jesus pleads your case before the Father when you fall into sin. He pleads His redeeming blood for you and for me. So don't let the enemy keep you down when you sin. Rush to God in prayer and point to the merits of Christ's shed blood on your behalf. It's not your goodness that grants you an audience in the courts of heaven; it is what Christ did for you on the Cross. His death allows you to come boldly to the throne of grace to find mercy and help in your time of need (Hebrews 4:16).

You have nothing of which to boast but you can boast in Christ and His Spirit because of what they accomplish in you and for you. "For when we were yet without strength, in due time Christ died for the ungodly" (Romans 5:6). "Not that we are sufficient of ourselves to think anything as of ourselves; but our sufficiency *is* of God," who "commendeth his love toward us, in that, while we were yet sinners, Christ died for us" (2 Corinthians 3:5; Romans 5:8).

Be encouraged. The more overpowering your trials, the more grace Christ bestows upon you. The weaker you are, the more power His Spirit exerts in your behalf. His pledge to you is, "Where sin abounded, grace did much more abound" (Romans 5:20). "My grace is sufficient for thee: for my strength is made perfect in weakness." Therefore, rejoice and be thankful for your weakness because the power and glory of Christ rest upon you. In the spiritual realm, when you are weak, through Christ, you are made strong (2 Corinthians 12:9-10).

Two warnings need to be sounded here. First, don't be tricked by the devil into thinking that God just looks away from sin as if He doesn't care. We've already seen that a child of God should not live in continuous sin. Don't presume to think that you can sin and live as you please and God will understand.

Paul had to warn the Roman Church of this error when he said, "What shall we say then? Shall we continue in sin, that grace may abound? God forbid. How shall we, that are dead to sin, live any longer therein?" (Romans 6:1-2)

Second, don't rely on your feelings and emotions. Your pattern of sin may cause you to feel uneasy about your salvation but remember we walk and live by faith—not by sight, feelings, or emotions (Romans 1:7; 2 Corinthians 5:7; Galatians 3:11; Hebrews 10:38). *Don't wait to feel you are forgiven and loved.* Don't wait to feel some special emotion that you now have God's approval. You have God's promises, and He will not and cannot lie (Numbers 23:19; 1 Samuel 15:29; Titus 1:2; Hebrews 6:18).

Treasure His pledges and live by faith. Feelings or no feelings, emotions or no emotions, do what is right because God said so, and that settles it. Live by principle, not by impulse. I love the saying used in our evangelistic meetings in Africa, "If the Bible says it, I believe it. And if I believe it, I will do it." Try applying that principle for the next seven days.

Are you not a Child of God? Didn't you profess that you're saved, sanctified, Holy Ghost filled, water baptized, and that Jesus is yours? Didn't you accept the gift of God which is eternal life through Jesus Christ our Lord? (Romans 6:23)

Wasn't it you who, *by faith,* gave your life to Jesus and received Him as your personal Savior? Don't you believe, "For God so loved the world, that he gave his only begotten Son, that whosoever believeth in him should not perish, but have everlasting life?" (John 3:16)

Then declare your strength right now. Say, "*In the* Lord have I righteousness and strength" (Isaiah 45:24). Don't settle for the mediocre Christianity that pitifully says, "*We fall down, but we get up.*" We have used that song as a crutch for too long. Say like Paul, "Therefore being justified by faith, we have peace with God through our Lord Jesus Christ" and because of this, you can do all things through Christ who strengthens you (Romans 5:1; Philippians 4:13).

Today, look away from self and look to Christ. Whatever instruction God has given you, He provides the power to do it. He says, "Look unto me, and be ye saved, all the ends of the earth: for I am God, and there is none else. I have sworn by myself, the word is gone out of my mouth in righteousness, and shall not return…In the Lord shall all the seed of Israel be justified, and shall glory" (Isaiah 45:22-23, 25). "There is therefore now no condemnation to them which are in Christ Jesus, who walk not after the flesh, but after the Spirit" (Romans 8:1).

Your enabler is Christ's Spirit, not your flesh. Don't let your flesh control you any longer. If you're going to succeed in the Christian journey, you must understand that it's "Not by might, nor by power, but **by my spirit,** saith the Lord of hosts" (Zechariah 4:6). "When the enemy shall come in like a flood, the Spirit of the Lord shall lift up a standard against him" (Isaiah 59:19).

If you *feel* destitute of the Holy Spirit, remember Christ promised the Comforter to His disciples. Don't go by feelings; ask for the promised blessing, in faith. "If ye then, being evil, know how to give good gifts unto your children:

**how much more** shall your heavenly Father give the Holy Spirit to them that ask him?" (Luke 11:13; Matthew 7:7-11) "But the Comforter, which is the Holy Ghost, whom the Father will send in my name, he shall teach you all things, and bring all things to your remembrance, whatsoever I have said unto you" (John 14:26). See also John 15:26; 16:7-11.

Right now you should be overflowing with power—it is your biblical mandate. "... Be filled with the Spirit. Walk in the Spirit, and ye shall not fulfill the lust of the flesh. ... be led of the Spirit." This is the antidote to all the sinful deeds of your flesh because "The fruit of the Spirit is love, joy, peace, longsuffering, gentleness, goodness, faith, meekness, temperance: against such there is no law." Use Cure #2 and watch your life transform before your eyes. Depend upon Christ and the Holy Spirit, because "They that are Christ's have crucified the flesh with the affections and lusts. If we live in the Spirit, let us also walk in the Spirit" (Ephesians 5:18; Galatians 5: 16, 18, 22-25).

The Holy Spirit is the only One who can keep us from living a life of sin. He empowers us to live holy lives, pleasing to God. When we are at our weakest and don't even know how to pray or what to pray for, "the Spirit also helpeth our infirmities: for we know not what we should pray for as we ought: but the Spirit itself maketh intercession for us with groanings which cannot be uttered. And he that searcheth the hearts knoweth what *is* the mind of the Spirit, because he maketh intercession for the saints according to *the will of* God" (Romans 8:26-27). With Jesus and the Holy Spirit, "... the righteousness of the law might be fulfilled in us, who walk not after the flesh, but after the Spirit" (Romans 8:4).

## CURE #3:  Surrender the Fight

In every battle, you need strategies. Some people keep losing battles but never sit down to analyze the tactics they're using. A wise person once said, "Insanity is doing the same thing over and over again but expecting different results." If you're constantly being defeated in a particular area, stop, think, and ask, "Why?"

Do you know your enemy? Do you know your allies? Do you know your strengths and weaknesses? Do you have the right game plan? Do you have the right weapons? These questions are important in warfare, and that's what you face everyday—spiritual warfare. A professional speaker frequently says, "If you are casual (in life, in war, etc.), you may become a casualty."

The Bible tells us "we wrestle not against flesh and blood, but against principalities, against powers, against the rulers of the darkness of this world, against spiritual wickedness in high places" (Ephesians 6:12). This is serious business. Satan is out to destroy you (1 Peter 5:8; John 10:10a), and he doesn't fight fairly. His tactics are "out of this world" but fear not, "we are not ignorant of his devices" (2 Corinthians 2:11).

Since this battle is spiritual, we must fight it on the spiritual plain and not on the physical or carnal plain. Some of us keep losing because we try to bring our earthly wisdom and logic into a spiritual battle and expect to defeat a spiritual being. Duh!

If you want to start winning again, you must surrender your 'know how' and use God's appointed weapons of warfare. "For though we walk in the flesh, we do not war after the flesh: (For the weapons of our warfare *are* not carnal, but mighty through God to the pulling down of strongholds" (2 Corinthians 10:3-4).

Remember we said earlier that the carnal mind cannot please God? The sinful flesh is an ally with the enemy and thus unreliable to combat your sinful propensities. Paul is telling us that our weapons are not carnal because we do not walk in the flesh. We walk in the Spirit. Therefore, your weapons must be spiritual and of the Holy Spirit.

You may be surprised at God's warfare strategies but they are effective nonetheless. They cast down imaginations and every high thing that exalts itself against the knowledge of God, and they bring every thought into captivity to the obedience of Christ (2 Corinthians 10:5). Let go of your current tactics, they've been failing you for too long. Cure #3 is about to change your spiritual condition.

I spent seven years and seven months in the U.S. Navy, and one thing I heard repeatedly from my superiors was, "If you're doing it *hard*, you're doing it wrong." Sometimes we think there must be a constant struggle and clashing to win, but that's not necessarily the case with God. They also frequently said, "KISS" it, Keep It Simple Sailor (they didn't say Sailor at the end, but it's appropriate for our study).

Remember this life principle (underline it): *Success is in simplicity; as soon as you depart from it, your strength (power) is gone.*

God's instructions may sometimes seem foolish, but "the foolishness of God is wiser than men; and the weakness of God is stronger than men. For ye see your calling, brethren, how that not many wise men after the flesh, not many mighty, not many noble, are called: But God hath chosen the foolish things of the world to confound the wise; and God hath chosen the weak things of the world to confound the things which are mighty; And base things of the world, and things which are despised, hath God chosen, yea, and things which are not, to bring to nought things that are: That no flesh should glory in his presence" (1 Corinthians 1:25-29).

God knows what He is doing. "Humble yourselves therefore under the mighty hand of God, that he may exalt you in due time" (1 Peter 5:6). Surrender the fight and use heaven's appointed strategies for spiritual warfare. God does not always use what *you* think because He says, "My thoughts are not your thoughts, neither are your ways my ways, saith the Lord. For *as* the heavens are higher than the earth, so are my ways higher than your ways, and my thoughts than your thoughts" (Isaiah 55:8-9).

When God wanted to destroy Jericho, He instructed the Israelites to simply walk around the walls once every day for six days and seven times on the seventh day, then blow the trumpets. The walls came tumbling down! Gideon put a massive army to flight with only 300 men, trumpets, and torches (as the Lord directed him). When no one knew how to handle the seven-year famine prophesied against Egypt, God used Joseph to instruct Pharaoh how to save the land. All Naaman had to do to be healed of leprosy was to obey the simple word of God to dip seven times in the "filthy" Jordan River. When the Moabites and Ammonites came against King Jehoshaphat and his people, God said they didn't even need to fight because the battle was His. All they had to *do* was go out against the enemy, but *stand still and see* the salvation of their God. They went out singing and praising the Lord and the battle was won! How is that for simplicity? (See Joshua 6:1-5; Judges 7; Genesis 41; 2 Kings 5:1-14; and 2 Chronicles 20:15-17.)

The following cure for mediocre Christianity may seem simple but that's why it's your key to success in Christ. I say to you "KISS" it, Keep It Simple, Saint. The *Surrender the Fight* cure has three actions you need to take. They can be done separately or combined, but it's better to combine them with a dose of prayer and the Holy Spirit. You're about to shatter all mediocrity.

**Action 1: Put on God's Armor**
Don't go to a gun fight with knives and a loin cloth. You'll be killed within seconds! Worse, don't show up for spiritual warfare dressed in carnal armor; you're defeated before you start. Instead, "Put on the whole armour of God, that ye may be able to stand against the wiles of the devil. Wherefore take unto you the whole armour of God, that ye may be able to withstand in the evil day, and having done all, to stand" (Ephesians 6:11, 13).

Notice Paul says to take the *whole* armor. Not most or some of the armor, but the whole armor! All the pieces must be worn lest you leave an important body part exposed. Cover it all—your private parts, chest, heart, abdomen, feet, hands, head, and your mind. What are these spiritual pieces in your armor? Truth, righteousness, gospel of peace, faith, Scripture, and prayer (Ephesians 6:14-18).

When all these pieces combine, even the weakest Christian will put Satan's entire army to flight. *Be armored in Christ* today, and go out to win battles in the Spirit.

**Action 2: Cling to the Vine**
We make it so complicated when it comes to dealing with temptation and sin. God has given us simple ingredients but we've added all kinds of ideas and ingredients to His recipe. Without Christ, we can do nothing. With Christ, all things are possible. The secret to bearing fruit is to simply *abide in Christ.*

Jesus said, "I am the true vine, and my Father takes care of the vineyard. He removes every one of my branches that doesn't produce fruit. He also prunes every branch that does produce fruit to make it produce more fruit. "You are already clean because of what I have told you. Live in me, and I will live in you. A branch cannot produce any fruit by itself. It has to stay attached to the vine. In the same way, *you cannot produce fruit unless you live in me.* "I am the vine. You are the branches. Those who live in me while I live in them will produce a lot of fruit. But you can't produce anything without me. Whoever doesn't live in me is thrown away like a branch and dries up. Branches like this are gathered, thrown into a fire, and burned. If you live in me and what I say lives in you, then ask for anything you want, and it will be yours. You give glory to my Father when you produce a lot of fruit and therefore show that you are my disciples. "I have loved you the same way the Father has loved me. So live in my love" (John 15:1-9 - GW).

I know you're frustrated that you can't seem to do the good you want to do but that's because you're not *abiding*. You have to surrender yourself, then yield your will and your way to God. Surrender every area of your life to the tender voice of the Holy Spirit. "Little children, abide in him; that, when he shall appear, we may have confidence, and not be ashamed before him at his coming" (1 John 2:28). Yield to God's pruning process, and you will be an overcomer.

God didn't make this complicated, did He? Just abide. How do you abide? Jesus told you how—live in Him, stay attached to Him, live in His Word and let His Word live in you, ask for spiritual blessings, and live in His love. That's it. Do these things, and you'll produce a lot of fruit.

**Action 3: Be a Sheep—A Real Sheep**
It's good to be a sheep! God's children are His sheep. He is the good Shepherd and will give His life for you (John 10:10b, 11, 14, 16-18). Because God is your Shepherd, you have everything you need; you shall not want for any good thing. Sing this beautiful Psalm of David for the next seven days and see how your attitudes to spiritual battles change.

"The Lord is my shepherd. I am never in need. He makes me lie down in green pastures. He leads me beside peaceful waters. He renews my soul. He guides me along the paths of righteousness for the sake of his name. Even though I walk through the dark valley of death, because you are with me, I fear no harm. Your rod and your staff give me courage. You prepare a banquet for me while my enemies watch. You anoint my head with oil. My cup overflows. Certainly, goodness and mercy will stay close to me all the days of my life, and I will remain in the Lord's house for days without end" (Psalm 23:1-6 - GW).

Who takes care of the sheep? Who leads the sheep besides green pastures and quiet (still) waters? Who guides the sheep along paths of righteousness? You're right. The Shepherd. It's all about the Shepherd. What's the role of the sheep? What does the sheep do? Like abiding in the Vine, to be a sheep, a real sheep, will require submission and humility on your part. All the sheep has to do is to be guided in paths of righteousness, to eat, drink, and do what the Shepherd asks. It's not the sheep's job to determine what it eats and drinks either. The Shepherd decides where and what the sheep eats and drinks and also the righteousness it partakes in.

So stop worrying about eating, drinking, and becoming righteous. Are you the Shepherd or are you a sheep? The Lord will ensure that you have your daily needs and become like Him in character. Your role as a sheep is simply to go where He leads, eat and drink what He provides, and absorb the righteousness He imputes and imparts. Depend upon Christ and the Holy Spirit. The good Shepherd will provide, protect, and lead you. Just follow Him and all will be well. Be a sheep—a real sheep. (See also Philippians 4:6-7 and Matthew 6:30-33.)

## CURE #4: Claim God's Promises

This prescription is my favorite for relinquishing mediocrity in every area of life. If I could give only one piece of advice to anyone, it would be "Rely on God's Promises." The greatest legacy I can leave my family, ministry, and the world is to teach people how to claim and depend on God's promises. Why are God's assurances so important to me? Because the only certainty in life is the certainty of God's promises.

People have grown so self-confident in what they know and the philosophies of the world that this can be called the Skeptical Age. The Bible calls such people "fools" (Psalm 14:1; 53:1). We are too proud of this so-called "Information Age." We need to humble ourselves before God.

"Let not the wise man glory in his wisdom, neither let the mighty man glory in his might, let not the rich man glory in his riches: But let him that glorieth glory in this, that he understandeth and knoweth me, that I am the Lord which exercise lovingkindness, judgment, and righteousness, in the earth: for in these things I delight, saith the Lord" (Jeremiah 9:23-24).

To apply Cure #4, self must step out of the picture. Hide yourself behind the Cross and let the Word of God be your guiding light. "Except a corn of wheat fall into the ground and die, it abideth alone: but if it dies, it bringeth forth much fruit" (John 12:24). If any man will come after me, let him deny himself, and take up his cross daily, and follow me. For whosoever will save his life shall lose it: but whosoever will lose his life for my sake, the same shall save it. For what is a man advantaged, if he gains the whole world, and loses himself, or be cast away? For whosoever shall be ashamed of me and of my words, of him shall the Son of man be ashamed, when he shall come in his own glory, and in his Father's, and of the holy angels" (Luke 9:23-26).

The promises of God are like silver bullets in spiritual warfare. They're lethal and life-giving at the same time—they cut and heal (Hebrews 4:12). We cannot live without them because "It is written, That man shall not live by bread alone, but by every word of God" (Luke 4:4; Matthew 4:4; Deuteronomy 8:3). Not by *some* of His words or even by *most* of His words, but by *every word* that proceeds from His mouth. Believe this, live this, and you'll be unstoppable!

How long then will you refuse to obey God? How long will you disobey the teachings of Christ because you won't do the good He instructs you to do? "How long halt ye between two opinions? If the Lord be God, follow him…" (1 Kings 18:21). There is no excuse for mediocrity; Cure #4, *Claiming God's Promises,* is what you need to take your stand for Christ.

If you're not claiming God's glorious promises by prayer and faith, then you're depriving yourself of a powerful antidote to spiritual mediocrity. God wants you to rise to excellence and live above the crowds. You can take His words to the bank because His note will cash out perfect—every time.

He's not like your friends and family who let you down and fail to live up to their promises. "God is not a man, that he should lie; neither the son of man, that he should repent:

hath he said, and shall he not do it? or hath he spoken, and shall he not make it good?" (Numbers 23:19). "And also the Strength of Israel will not lie nor repent: for he is not a man, that he should repent" (1 Samuel 15:29). "In hope of eternal life, which God, that cannot lie, promised before the world began" (Titus 1:2). "That by two immutable things, in which it was impossible for God to lie" (Hebrews 6:18).

Bask in the certainty of His promises to you right now. Repeat them over and over again. Put them up in your home, office, and surroundings. Memorize them, write them and rewrite them. Put them in a song. Let the promises of God be your meditations morning, noon, and night. Do this with the same faith you had when you first accepted God's free gift of salvation.

Unlike man's flimsy promises, whose word is only good so far as his ability to perform, God's word contains the power within itself to accomplish what it pledges to accomplish. He doesn't need to lift a finger to carry out His words. Just the fact that he spoke it means it shall be done (in His time and in His way).

Here's a snapshot of God's powerful words. "My covenant will I not break, nor alter the thing that is gone out of my lips. Once have I sworn by my holiness that I will not lie unto David. His seed shall endure forever, and his throne as the sun before me. It shall be established forever as the moon, and as a faithful witness in heaven." Selah (Psalm 89:33-37).

"So shall my word be that goeth forth out of my mouth: it shall not return unto me void, but it shall accomplish that which I please, and it shall prosper in the thing whereto I sent it" (Isaiah 55:11).

"By the word of the Lord were the heavens made; and all the host of them by the breath of his mouth. For he spake, and it was done; he commanded, and it stood fast" (Psalm 33:6, 9).

To claim a Bible promise is really simple. You have to exercise faith in God and His ability and willingness to do what He has promised (see Hebrews 11:6 and Psalm 111:3-8). You must ask God (in prayer) for what He has promised. Believe that He hears you and that He will do what He promised. Then claim or receive the promised blessing. And then thank God for hearing and answering your petitions. Jesus assures you, "What things soever ye desire, when ye pray, believe that ye receive them, and ye shall have them" (Mark 11:24).

Go to your Bible and find promises that pertain to whatever you need help with. Meet the conditions given in the promise and experience the blessings of obeying God. You can study more about claiming God's promises in my book, *The Certainty of God's Promises,* available at 7smr.org, StrategicSecrets.com, Barnesandnoble.com, and Amazon.com.

Here are some promises to get you started that will revitalize your Christian experience. But start compiling your own list of Bible promises that speak to your unique situation and watch your relationship with Christ grow exponentially.

**Promises about Faith**
Have faith in God. For verily I say unto you, That whosoever shall say unto this mountain, Be thou removed, and be thou cast into the sea; and shall not doubt in his heart, but shall

believe that those things which he saith shall come to pass; he shall have whatsoever he saith (Mark 11:22-23).

Now unto him that is able to do exceeding abundantly above all that we ask or think, according to the power that worketh in us (Ephesians 3:20).

Jesus said unto him, "If thou canst believe, all things are possible to him that believeth" (Mark 9:23).

But without faith it is impossible to please him: for he that cometh to God must believe that he is, and that he is a rewarder of them that diligently seek him (Hebrews 11:6).

**Promises for Forgiveness**
Seek ye the Lord while he may be found, call ye upon him while he is near: Let the wicked forsake his way, and the unrighteous man his thoughts: and let him return unto the Lord, and he will have mercy upon him; and to our God, for he will abundantly pardon (Isaiah 55:6-7).

He that covereth his sins shall not prosper: but whoso confesseth and forsaketh them shall have mercy (Proverbs 28:13).

If we confess our sins, he is faithful and just to forgive us our sins, and to cleanse us from all unrighteousness (1 John 1:9).

That if thou shalt confess with thy mouth the Lord Jesus, and shalt believe in thine heart that God hath raised him from the dead, thou shalt be saved. For with the heart man believeth unto righteousness; and with the mouth confession is made unto salvation. For the scripture saith, Whosoever believeth on him shall not be ashamed (Romans 10:9-11).

**Promises for Strength**
God *is* our refuge and strength, a very present help in trouble. Therefore will not we fear, though the earth be removed, and though the mountains be carried into the midst of the sea; Though the waters thereof roar and be troubled, though the mountains shake with the swelling thereof. Selah (Psalm 46:1-3).

The Lord *is* on my side; I will not fear: what can man do unto me? (Psalms 118:6).

But the Lord is faithful, who shall stablish you, and keep you from evil (2 Thessalonians 3:3).

Fear thou not; for I am with thee: be not dismayed; for I am thy God: I will strengthen thee; yea, I will help thee; yea, I will uphold thee with the right hand of my righteousness (Isaiah 41:10).

**Promises for Peace**
Be careful for nothing; but in everything by prayer and supplication with thanksgiving let your requests be made known unto God. And the peace of God, which passeth all understanding, shall keep your hearts and minds through Christ Jesus (Philippians 4:6-7).

Casting all your care upon him; for he careth for you (1 Peter 5:7).

I laid me down and slept; I awaked; for the Lord sustained me. I will not be afraid of ten thousands of people, that have set themselves against me round about (Psalm 3:5-6).

Peace I leave with you, my peace I give unto you: not as the world giveth, give I unto you. Let not your heart be troubled, neither let it be afraid (John 14:27).

**Promises for Protection**
What shall we then say to these things? If God be for us, who can be against us? He that spared not his own Son, but delivered him up for us all, how shall he not with him also freely give us all things? (Romans 8:31-32).

Because thou hast made the Lord, which is my refuge, even the most High, thy habitation; There shall no evil befall thee, neither shall any plague come nigh thy dwelling. For he shall give his angels charge over thee, to keep thee in all thy ways. They shall bear thee up in their hands, lest thou dash thy foot against a stone. (Psalm 91:9-12).

In righteousness shalt thou be established: thou shalt be far from oppression; for thou shalt not fear: and from terror; for it shall not come near thee. (Isaiah 54:14)

Because he hath set his love upon me, therefore will I deliver him: I will set him on high, because he hath known my name. He shall call upon me, and I will answer him: I will be with him in trouble; I will deliver him, and honour him. With long life will I satisfy him, and shew him my salvation (Psalm 91:14-16).

## Promises of God's Provision

But my God shall supply all your need according to his riches in glory by Christ Jesus (Philippians 4:19).

And we know that all things work together for good to them that love God, to them who are the called according to his purpose (Romans 8:28).

Trust in the Lord, and do good; so shalt thou dwell in the land, and verily thou shalt be fed. Delight thyself also in the Lord; and he shall give thee the desires of thine heart. Commit thy way unto the Lord; trust also in him; and he shall bring it to pass (Psalm 37:3-5).

Believe in the Lord your God, so shall ye be established; believe his prophets, so shall ye prosper (2 Chronicles 20:20b).

## Promises of Success

He giveth power to the faint; and to them that have no might he increaseth strength. Even the youths shall faint and be weary, and the young men shall utterly fall: But they that wait upon the Lord shall renew their strength; they shall mount up with wings as eagles; they shall run, and not be weary; and they shall walk, and not faint (Isaiah 40:29-31).

For promotion cometh neither from the east, nor from the west, nor from the south. But God is the judge: he putteth down one, and setteth up another (Psalm 75:6-7).

Through God we shall do valiantly: for he it is that shall tread down our enemies. (Psalm 60:12)

Only be thou strong and very courageous, that thou mayest observe to do according to all the law, which Moses my servant commanded thee: turn not from it to the right hand or to the left, that thou mayest prosper whithersoever thou goest. (Joshua 1:7)

## CURE #5: Use God's Seven-Step Plan for Victory

If you feel like all chips are down and you still can't seem to break the *"We-fell-down-but-we-can't-get-up"* syndrome, I have a remedy for you. This cure works when you have no other option. Mediocrity cannot stand against God's Seven-Step Plan for Victory. To use this cure effectively, follow these seven steps:

### Step 1. Choose Not to Sin
Say a positive "NO!" when sin comes knocking on your door. "… Choose you this day whom ye will serve" (Joshua 24:15).

### Step 2. Keep the Faith
Don't forget that you were saved by faith and therefore you are justified, sanctified, and will be gloried because of faith. "For we are saved by hope: but hope that is seen is not hope: for what a man seeth, why doth he yet hope for? But if we hope for that we see not, then do we with patience wait for it" (Romans 8:24-25).

### Step 3. Make No Provision for the Flesh
Have a game plan. Don't expose yourself to things that cause you to fall. Remove anything that feeds your craving for sin. If you have a problem with pornography, don't visit the magazine shops; put a filter on your computer. Be wise, "… put ye on the Lord Jesus Christ, and make not provision for the flesh, to fulfill the lusts thereof" (Romans 13:14).

### Step 4. Consider Yourself Dead to Sin

Dead people can't smoke, drink, curse, or get angry. "Knowing this, that our old man is crucified with him, that the body of sin might be destroyed, that henceforth we should not serve sin. For he that is dead is freed from sin. Likewise reckon ye also yourselves to be dead indeed unto sin, but alive unto God through Jesus Christ our Lord" (Romans 6:6-7, 11).

### Step 5. Claim Your Victory and Power in Christ

You are a conqueror through Christ (Romans 8:37). Declare your standing in the face of the enemy and start praising God for what He has already done for and through you. "But thanks be to God, which giveth us the victory through our Lord Jesus Christ. Therefore, my beloved brethren, be ye steadfast, unmovable, always abounding in the work of the Lord, forasmuch as ye know that your labour is not in vain in the Lord" (1 Corinthians 15:57-58).

### Step 6. Take God's Exit Plan

Don't reason with temptation. Flee as soon as the Holy Spirit reveals the attack to you. Take the exit. "There hath no temptation taken you but such as is common to man: but God is faithful, who will not suffer you to be tempted above that ye are able; but will with the temptation also make a way to escape, that ye may be able to bear it" (1 Corinthians 10:13).

### Step 7. Ask for Help

You have brothers and sisters available to help you on the Christian journey. You don't have to go it alone. Reach out for help, it may be the difference between victory and defeat.

"Two are better than one; because they have a good reward for their labour. For if they fall, the one will lift up his fellow: but woe to him that is alone when he falleth; for he hath not another to help him up. Again, if two lie together, then they have heat: but how can one be warm alone? And if one prevail against him, two shall withstand him; and a threefold cord is not quickly broken" (Ecclesiastes 4:9-12).

# CURE # 6: Be Transformed by Renewing Your Mind

These last two cures are unlike the previous five. They will only work if you work them. God created us with free will and choice, that's why Adam and Eve had the liberty to disobey Him. God does not take this right away from you. You must make a choice to implement these last two cures. No one will force you; it's all up to you.

You may be thinking, "Why doesn't God just *make* me to do what He wants me to do? Or, "If God wanted me to really have the victory, He would do it for me; I guess it may not be His will." This is a typical cop-out tactic for many people. If that were the case, then why doesn't God brush your teeth, comb your hair, tie your shoe laces, pick up the spoon to feed you, and use the bathroom for you? There are some things you must do for yourself, there's no way around that. God will not do those basic things for you since He has equipped you to do them.

Likewise, most of God's promises are conditional—there are conditions to their fulfillment. Wherever you find a promise in Scripture, there's usually God's part and your part. Your part is the condition upon which the promise is based. God will make a claim, an order, or a command, which He backs up with a guarantee, or He gives full assurance for the individual to exercise his or her faith based solely on His promise. Then you have the final result of the promise—call it the reward, the answer, or the blessing realized.

Cure #6, *Be Transformed by Renewing Your Mind* is a program to recondition the way you think and act. It's important because the current state of your mind is producing habits which you now hate. You see, your thoughts influence your words, which decide your actions, which create your habits, which form your character, which determine your destiny.

The battle is for the mind! Satan well knows that if he can program your mind with all the filth of this world, then there's no way you can ever win battles against him. *If you can win on the mental battlefield, then* **victory is certain**.

Some people keep falling because they're trying to change habits. They see a weak spot in their character and they set out to change it, only to see another problem area pop up and then another until utter frustration takes over. That's putting out fires. That's not getting to the root cause of the problem, the source of the fire.

If the output is bad, don't focus all your energies trying to fix the output. If the results you're getting are not what you expected, don't try harder to improve the end results. If you want to do good but keep doing bad, then *trying* harder would only make it worse, because effort is the reason you cannot do the good you need to do.

There's a popular saying that goes something like "garbage in, garbage out." It is generally used as a negative connotation, and rightly so. However, we can add to this saying and learn a powerful system for overcoming mediocrity in every area of life. How about: "input equals output; what you put in is what you get out; truth in, truth out." You get the point.

Based on this reasoning, if the output you're getting is unacceptable (instead of doing the good you want to do, you end up doing what you hate), then change the input. If your behavior is not commensurate with that of a TRUE Christian, then don't just seek behavior modification, that's not the problem, change the input! *If you really want transformation you must change your information.*

Why do you think a man commits a criminal act? If he is brought to trial, what will the court try to figure out? The lawyer will try to figure out *why* this person did what he did—what was he thinking? Why is this information important? "For as he thinketh in his heart, so *is* he" (Proverbs 23:7). If he thinks evil in his heart, his words and actions will be evil. He's just acting out what was in his mind already—the motives.

When should he have been arrested for his crime? When was the crime actually committed? Did he commit the crime the moment it was carried out? Certainly not. He committed the crime *before* the physical act took place. He was a criminal *before* he did the criminal act (that could have been a long time or a short time). This is what legal folks call pre-meditated acts. So if he premeditated the crime, then the crime already took place *before* the physical act. It took place in his mind.

That's why Jesus taught this allegory, "There is nothing from without a man, that entering into him can defile him: but the things which come out of him, those are they that defile the man." When He entered into the house after being with the people, His disciples asked the meaning of the parable. He said, "Are ye so without understanding also? Do ye not perceive, that whatsoever thing from without entereth into the man, it cannot defile him; Because it entereth not into his heart, but into the belly, and goeth out into the draught, purging all meats? And he said, That which cometh out of the man, that defileth the man. For from *within, out of the heart (mind) of men*, proceed evil thoughts, adulteries, fornications, murders, thefts, covetousness, wickedness, deceit, lasciviousness, an evil eye, blasphemy, pride, foolishness: All these evil things come from within, and defile the man" (Mark 7:15-23).

The same thing applies to you and me. You are not a hypocrite when you do double-faced acts; you were already a hypocrite in your heart or mind. What people see is a mere reflection of what's taking place in your heart (mind). That's why the saying, "actions speak louder than words" weighs a ton of truth. Jesus defends this point when He said, "Whosoever looketh on a woman to lust after her hath committed adultery with her *already* in his heart" (Matthew 5:28).

Let's see if the Apostle Paul can help us apply Treatment #6 to mediocre Christianity. Look at Romans 12:1-2: "I beseech you therefore, brethren, by the mercies of God, that ye present your bodies a living sacrifice, holy, acceptable unto God, which is your reasonable service. And be not conformed to this world: but be ye transformed by the renewing of your mind, that ye may prove what is that good, and acceptable, and perfect, will of God."

Notice he did not say to be transformed by renewing the flesh or the renewing of your habits. You cannot renew the sinful nature! It must die daily. Crucifixion is the only suitable way to rid yourself of the sinful nature. But if you desire transformation, it begins with the heart and mind. The battle is in the mind.

Go back to Romans 7 where we studied *The Root Problem of Just "Knowing."* You recall that Paul eloquently described the reason why your habits betray you. It is because sin is still present in your flesh. He paints the struggle between the spirit and the carnal nature, between his mind and his flesh.

Before he cries out bitterly in verse 24, he gives a clue to why he is a captive to the law of sin in his members (habits, actions, body, activities, etc). "But I see another law in my members, *warring against the law of my mind,* and bringing me into captivity to the law of sin which is in my members" (Romans 7:23).

Where is the war taking place? Where is the citadel of the problem? You guessed it, in his mind. After his bitter cry, we find another clue to why he is a captive to the law of sin in his members. "With the mind I myself serve the law of God; *but with the flesh the law of sin*" (Romans 7:25b). The BBE renders it, "So *I am obedient to God's standards with my mind,* but I am obedient to sin's standards with my corrupt nature."

This is a powerful and life-transforming piece of wisdom. Seize it. If you are going to change your lifestyle habits and be free from being a *professing* Christian, you must reprogram your mind. Be transformed by the renewing of your mind. "Be renewed in the spirit of your mind. ... Put on the new man, which is renewed in knowledge after the image of him that created him: Let this mind be in you, which was also in Christ Jesus" (Ephesians 4:23; Colossians 3:10; Philippians 2:5).

This cure is an extreme mind make-over to help you have and maintain the mind of Christ. To be transformed means to renovate, change, alter, revamp, and restore your old way of thinking into the way Christ thought.

**How to Reprogram Your Mind**
First, know that it's not through philosophy or man-made gimmicks. The flesh has failed you too many times. Remember, "The weapons of our warfare are not carnal, but mighty through God to the pulling down of strongholds. Casting down imaginations, and every high thing that exalteth itself against the knowledge of God..." (2 Corinthians 10:4-5b).

Cure #6 is anti-carnal. If you want to be more like Christ, you'll need to use the tools He authorizes: namely, His Word. "Thy word is a lamp unto my feet, and a light unto my path" (Psalm 119:105). "Set your affection on things above, not on things on the earth" (Colossians 3:2). Here are seven biblical Keys to renewing your mind.

**Key #1: Fill Your Mind with the Knowledge of God**
Learn about God—His character, His love, His requirements, and His ways. We often fall short of God's ideal because we don't really *know* Him. Every morning, get into His Word and get the right picture of your heavenly Father. "Study to shew thyself approved unto God, a workman that needeth

not to be ashamed, rightly dividing the word of truth" (2 Timothy 2:15).

"… Desire that ye might be filled with the knowledge of his will in all wisdom and spiritual understanding; that ye might walk worthy of the Lord unto all pleasing, being fruitful in every good work, and increasing in the knowledge of God; strengthened with all might, according to his glorious power, unto all patience and longsuffering with joyfulness" (Colossians 1:9-11).

**Key #2: Meditate Daily on God's Words**
When you read or listen to Scripture, think about it. Ponder what God is saying to you *personally.* How can you apply it? How can you share it? How will you change in light of what you read or heard? "This book of the law shall not depart out of thy mouth; but thou shalt meditate therein day and night…" (Joshua 1:8a).

"But his delight *is* in the law of the Lord; and in his law doth he meditate day and night" (Psalm 1:2-3). "O how love I thy law! It *is* my meditation all the day. I have more understanding than all my teachers: for thy testimonies *are* my meditation" (Psalm 119:97, 99).

**Key #3: Practice the Teachings of God**
Daily live out what you learn in Scripture. Practice makes perfect. Could that be the reason you're still not perfect? God promises to perfect that which concerns you but if you don't apply His *perfecting* methods, then how can you be perfected? "Wherewithal shall a young man cleanse

his way? By taking heed thereto according to thy word" (Psalm 119:9).

"... Observe to do according to all that is written therein: for then thou shalt make thy way prosperous, and then thou shalt have good success" (Joshua 1:8). "I understand more than the ancients, because I keep thy precepts. I have refrained my feet from every evil way, that I might keep thy word" (Psalm 119:100-101). "Those things, which ye have both learned, and received, and heard, and seen in me, do: and the God of peace shall be with you" (Philippians 4:9).

**Key #4: Memorize the Word of God**
The more you get the Word into your heart and mind, the stronger you will be. The Word is your spiritual food, commit key passages to memory. This was part of King David's and the Apostle Paul's battle plan. Start with verses you like, maybe the promises listed in Cure #4. As you get better, try memorizing a chapter, then an entire book. Your mind will never be the same. "Thy word have I hid in mine heart, that I might not sin against thee" (Psalm 119:11). "Moreover, brethren, I declare unto you the gospel which I preached unto you, which also ye have received, and wherein ye stand; By which also ye are saved, if ye keep in memory what I preached unto you" (1 Corinthians 15:1-2).

**Key #5: Speak and Sing the Word of God**
"While it is true that words express thoughts, it is also true that thoughts follow words. If we would give more expression to our faith, rejoice more in the blessings that we know we have,—the great mercy and love of God,—we should

have more faith and greater joy" (*The Ministry of Healing*, pp. 252-253).

"Speaking to yourselves in psalms and hymns and spiritual songs, singing and making melody in your heart to the Lord; giving thanks always for all things unto God and the Father in the name of our Lord Jesus Christ" (Ephesians 5:19-20). "God ... calleth those things which be not as though they were" (Romans 4:17).

**Key #6: Subject Every Thought to the Word of God**
*Guard well the avenues to your mind.* Every thought that comes to mind should not dwell in the mind nor find expression in words and deeds. Ask yourself, "How does this thought line up with the Word?" "Does this thought fit me as a child of God?" "Would Jesus approve of such a thought?"

Bring every thought into captivity to the obedience of Christ (2 Corinthians 10:5b). Say, "I hate vain thoughts: but thy law do I love" (Psalm 119:113). "Commit thy works unto the Lord, and thy thoughts shall be established" (Proverbs 16:3).

**Key #7: Change the Quality of Your Information**
Since negative in equals negative out, then put positive in and you should get positive out. *Think the way you want to be and the day will come when you will be the way you think.* Instead of the junk you've been putting into your mind, read, watch, listen, speak, and meditate on "Whatsoever things are true, whatsoever things are honest, whatsoever things are just, whatsoever things are pure, whatsoever things are lovely, whatsoever things are of good report; if there be any

virtue, and if there be any praise, think on these things" (Philippians 4:8).

If you really want transformation, change the quality of your information. "Give diligence to make your calling and election sure: If you do these things, you shall never fall" (2 Peter 1:10).

# CURE #7: Apply the Discipline of Action

*Discipline* has a bad connotation to most people. It sounds big and harsh, but it simply means to exercise control, restraint, and obedience. Mediocre living is a result of an ill-disciplined mind and habits. People cannot or will not restrain themselves from doing harmful things. People are obese and addicted to wrong things generally because they lack self-discipline. They refuse to exercise their will in controlling their appetites and lower passions.

That's why it's fitting to end this series on Cure #7. I want to help you *Apply the Discipline of Action.* There's no better time to start than right now. To be disciplined is to do the things you need to do *when* you need to do them. It's truly not as hard as you think. Implement these "Seven Strategic Secrets to Develop Self Discipline," and mediocrity will be a thing of the past.

**Strategic Secret 1: Ask God for Power and Wisdom to Be Disciplined**
Follow the example of one of my fitness heroes, the late *Jack LaLanne*. Many people know him as the pioneer of fitness gyms in America, host of a 34-year health and fitness TV show, and doing 1,033 pushups in 23 minutes, and swimming a mile attached to 70 boats filled with 70 people on his $70^{th}$ birthday. Jack disciplined himself to faithfully rise early in the morning (5:00 am) to exercise for 2½ hours! He did this every day until his death in 2011.

It was not always this way for Jack. He was a sickly skinny kid with pimples and boils but his life changed when he prayed to God for power to overcome his unhealthy lifestyle. Here's the simple prayer he whispered that turned him into a fitness guru, "Please give me the will-power and intestinal fortitude to refrain from eating wrong, lifeless, dead foods when the urge comes over me. God, please give me the strength to exercise when I don't feel like it."

If you want to be disciplined, ask God for power and wisdom. "He giveth power to the faint; and to *them that have* no might he increaseth strength" (Isaiah 40:29). "If any of you lack wisdom, let him ask of God, who giveth to all men liberally, and upbraideth not; and it shall be given him" (James 1:5).

**Strategic Secret 2:   Exercise Full Control of Your Will**
God has already given you self-discipline if you are His child. Exercise it! "The fruit of the Spirit is love, joy, peace... self-control" (Galatians 5:22-23). Benjamin Disraeli once said, "Nothing can destroy the will of a people." So long as they have the will to fight, nothing can defeat a man or woman who makes up his or her mind to win. *Before* the next temptation comes, *will* yourself to be a conqueror. *Will* your way to victory. Like freedom of choice, you can choose to be disciplined.

God has not given you the spirit of fear; but He has given you the spirit of power, and of love, and of self-discipline (2 Timothy 1:7). Take authority over your desires. Command your mind and body to behave—to do what you know is right and good to do.

**Strategic Secret 3: Learn More and You Will Be More**
People love to quote Hosea, saying, "My people are destroyed for lack of knowledge." However, in this day and age, people are *not* destroyed for lack of knowledge; they're destroyed for lack of *doing*—a lack of adequately applying knowledge. After all, Daniel prophesied that in the last days, "knowledge shall be increased" (Daniel 12:4). When Hosea said they were destroyed for lack of knowledge he explains why, "because *thou hast rejected knowledge,* I will also reject thee, that thou shalt be no priest to me: seeing *thou hast forgotten the law of thy God,* I will also forget thy children" (Hosea 4:6).

Knowledge is readily available but you must purposely set out to acquire and develop it. To learn more, watch, read, listen, memorize, research, study, and mediate on God's Word. As you learn more, you'll be equipped and empowered to do and to be more.

**Strategic Secret 4: Just Do It!**
You can't escape this great NIKE® slogan. After you've learned, nothing happens until you apply—practice, live out, prove, test, and model your newfound knowledge. All famous athletes spend hours practicing, day in and day out. They develop their skills to the highest degree of perfection. This is what the Apostle Paul meant when he said, "Those things, which ye have both learned, and received, and heard, and seen in me, *do*: and the God of peace shall be with you" (Philippians 4:9).

*Just Do It* is akin to the principle of Sowing and Reaping. The results you get will be proportionate to the effort you put in. "He which soweth sparingly shall reap also sparingly;

and he which soweth bountifully shall reap also bountifully" (2 Corinthians 9:6).

This is not righteousness by works, but you have some work to do in overcoming sinful tendencies. You are where you are today because of the accumulated actions and habits you formed over the years. Overcoming will also take a new set of accumulated actions and habits. "Whatsoever a man soweth, that shall he also reap. For he that soweth to his flesh shall of the flesh reap corruption; but he that soweth to the Spirit shall of the Spirit reap life everlasting. And let us not be weary in well doing: for in due season we shall reap, if we faint not" (Galatians 6:7-9).

**Strategic Secret 5: Teach your Heart and Lips to Praise and Thank God**

Jesus made a bold statement that you should consider. "How can ye, being evil, speak good things? for out of the abundance of the heart the mouth speaketh. A good man out of the good treasure of the heart bringeth forth good things: and an evil man out of the evil treasure bringeth forth evil things. But I say unto you, That every idle word that men shall speak, they shall give account thereof in the day of judgment. For by thy words thou shalt be justified, and by thy words thou shalt be condemned" (Matthew 12:34-37).

Words are powerful. They can create and destroy at the same time. "Death and life are in the power of the tongue: and they that love it shall eat the fruit thereof" (Proverbs 18:21). "Therewith bless we God, even the Father; and therewith curse we men, which are made after the similitude of God.

Out of the same mouth proceedeth blessing and cursing. My brethren, these things ought not so to be" (James 3:9-10).

You must therefore teach your heart and lips to praise and thank God and to speak holy. Your words have a telling influence on your emotions and decisions. Words decide actions, which form habits, which form character, and which ultimately determine your destiny.

*Speak the way you want to be and the day will come when you will be the way you speak.* Call those good things which are not yet in your life as though they were (Romans 4:17).

Talk more of joy, optimism, and positive things that you want to experience. Learn to rejoice in all things (Philippians 4:4; 1 Thessalonians 5:16). Impart grace by talking faith and hope. "Let no corrupt communication proceed out of your mouth, but that which is good to the use of edifying, that it may minister grace unto the hearers" (Ephesians 4:29).

**Strategic Secret 6: Establish a Daily Success Routine**
*Your success is determined by your daily routine.* Tell me what your daily habits are and I can predict the kind of success you are having and will have. God is a God of order (1 Corinthians 14:40) so you should be a person of order and discipline.

Make a schedule that you follow daily. Include: prayer, Bible study, exercise, good nutrition, meaningful service, time for family and friends, rest, and reflection. Do these things, and I guarantee you will develop a habit of doing things you need to do when you need to do them.

"...Study to be quiet, and to do your own business, and to work with your own hands, as we commanded you; That ye may walk honestly toward them that are without, and that ye may have lack of nothing" (1 Thessalonians 4:11-12).

**Strategic Secret 7: Never, Never, Never Give up**
On October 29, 1941, Winston Churchill delivered a profound speech to the boys of Harrow, his old school. I believe it may have been one of most powerful speeches ever given. Churchill's address contains a powerful message for you. He uttered these famous words on that memorable day, "Never give in. Never give in. Never, never, never, never--in nothing, great or small, large or petty--never give in, except to convictions of honor and good sense. Never yield to force. Never yield to the apparently overwhelming might of the enemy."

Churchill gave those boys a simple poignant lesson that if they took it to heart, they could never fail at any good thing in life. You can only be defeated when you choose to be defeated. The righteous may fall down seven times, but he gets back up and keeps moving (Proverbs 24:16). This is the key to living boldly for Christ. No matter how hard it gets, never give in, never give up. Never settle for mediocrity and a few paltry achievements. Never let Satan trample all over you. Keep on keeping on. Press the battle to the gates (Isaiah 28:6). Never, never, *never* give up.

"Not as though I had already attained, either were already perfect: but I follow after, if that I may apprehend that for which also I am apprehended of Christ Jesus. Brethren, I count not myself to have apprehended: but this one thing I do, forgetting those things which are behind, and reaching forth unto those things which are before, I press toward the mark for the prize of the high calling of God in Christ Jesus" (Philippians 3:12-14).

The message of this book comes with a sense of urgency because we are living in these last days, and perilous times are upon us (2 Timothy 3:1). The lines of demarcation between the righteous and the wicked are becoming increasingly clear.

Are you selfish, greedy, conceited, boastful, proud, insulting, irreverent, disobedient to your parents and others in authority, ungrateful, unholy, unloving, unforgiving, slanderous, lacking self-control, violent, always angry, despising what is good and right, treacherous, reckless, swollen with pride, and loving entertainment more than loving God? (2 Timothy 3:2-4).

Pause here. Be honest with yourself. How many of these traits are still present in your life? Go back through the list and put a check mark against each trait you know you still have present with you.

Don't fool yourself or be fooled by people who only have a form of godliness, who know the religious lingo but are not transformed into Christ's character. Their Christianity is not real. Such people deny the power of God, and the need for them to change. Have nothing to do with such persons, especially if it's yourself—your sinful self (2 Timothy 1:5).

"What is the test of true religion? **Knowing and doing the will of God**, in accordance with every word that proceedeth out of the mouth of God" (*Manuscript Releases Volume 20 [Nos. 1420-1500],* p. 68).

If you've carefully read this book, you know what a true Christian should be like. If after this spiritual diagnosis you do not resemble Christ, then use the suggestions given in this chapter. Apply any or all these Seven Cures for Mediocre Christianity and you will experience the full power of God in your daily life. Don't be your old self. Don't be like those who are "ever learning, and never able to come to a knowledge of the truth" (2 Timothy 3:1-7).

The ways of God are not hard. Simply: Remember who you are and Whose you are; Depend upon Christ and the Holy Spirit; Surrender the struggle; Claim God's promises by prayer and faith; Use God's seven-step plan for victory, Be transformed by renewing your mind; and Discipline your heart to act upon God's instructions. That's it—**Cures for Mediocre Christianity.**

> "Now that you *know* these things,
> blessed (happy) are you if you *do* them"
> (John 13:17).

# BONUS CURE FOR MEDIOCRE CHRISTIANITY

## *Love-The More Excellent Way*

This is **the most important key** to spiritual success! It is by far the greatest principle. If you want to truly become more like Christ on a daily basis, choose love—the more excellent way. Everything hinges on obedience to God's instructions and without it, no other Christian act would have meaning but *love is the bedrock of Christianity.* It is the only way that people will know you're a Christian—by your love for one another. Love fulfills the law and is greater than all other qualities under the sun.

Love must be first and foremost *Christ-centered* (as seen in the first four of the Ten Commandments—also called the First and Greatest Commandment) and *other people directed* (as seen in the last six of the Ten Commandments—also called the Second Greatest Commandment). The professed Christian who is low in love will be high in fault-finding. He or she will not make a good "fisher-of-men." Furthermore, if your spiritual love tank is low, you will not be able to love the Lord your God with all your heart, soul, and mind, nor love your neighbor as yourself. "On these two commandments hang all the law and the prophets (and the Golden Rule principle)" (Matthew 22:37-40).

This is one of the reasons why there are many lifeless and problematic churches today—people have no love. Jesus predicted that one of the signs to know His second coming is near is that "the love of many will wax (grow) cold" (Matthew 24:12).

Love is a litmus test of true Christ-like living. When you love, you do things to please the one you profess to love. A man shows by his actions how much he loves his wife. He wants to please her and the same is true of the wife to her husband. Children do what is good and right because they love their parents. Therefore, whenever you disobey God, what you are really saying is, "I have little love for my heavenly Father." True love on the other hand, will motivate you to get rid of besetting sins (Hebrews 12:1, 2) and love others just the same as God loves and treats us.

It is indeed a high calling to exhibit the spirit of true Christian love. If God would have us love even our enemies, how much greater should the body of Christ demonstrate love for each other? Not only are we to let brotherly love continue, we're also to, "Let love be without deceit. Be haters of what is evil; keep your minds fixed on what is good. Be kind to one another with a brother's love, putting others before yourselves in honor. Be tenderhearted, forgiving one another, even as God for Christ's sake hath forgiven you. Put on therefore, as the elect of God, holy and beloved, bowels of mercies, kindness, humbleness of mind, meekness, longsuffering; Forbearing one another, and forgiving one another, if you have a quarrel against any: even as Christ forgave you, forgive them freely. Above all these things put on charity, which is the bond of perfectness" (Hebrews 13:1; Romans 12:9-10—BBE; Ephesians 4:32; Colossians 3:12-14).

Keep in mind that pure love is a work of the Holy Spirit within. But don't despair, "if our heart condemns us, God is greater than our heart, and knoweth all things" (1 John 3:20). If you are a true born-again believer, God has already put His love within you, as a gift—a fruit of His Spirit (Galatians 5:22; 2 Timothy 1:7).

In all Christian affairs, love then is the operative word. Obedience may be the key but there can be no genuine obedience without genuine love. How then do you show love for God and your fellow man? How does love enable you to keep God's commandments? First, you must desire and seek the most excellent of all gifts—love. God is love and we love Him because He first loved us. Since He loves us, we ought to sincerely love others (1 John 4:8b, 19, 7).

Second, ask God to fill you with His Spirit and love. Seek for this with all your heart, mind, soul, and strength—which comes from Christ. Apply the following daily and consistently:

- "Be in debt for nothing, but to have love for one another: for he who has love for his neighbour has kept all the law (*has fulfilled the law*)" (Romans 13:8 - BBE).

- "Love does no wrong to his neighbour, so love makes the law complete (*fulfills the law*)" (Romans 13:10 - BBE).

- Love the brethren because if you don't love your brother, you abide in death (1 John 3: 14).

- "Whosoever hateth his brother is a murderer: and ye know that no murderer hath eternal life abiding in him" (1 John 3: 15).

- "Hereby perceive we the love of God, because he laid down his life for us: and we ought to lay down our lives for the brethren" (1 John 3: 16).

- "…Whoso hath this world's good, and seeth his brother have need, and shutteth up his bowels of compassion from him, how dwelleth the love of God in him?" (1 John 3: 17).

- "… Love not in word, neither in tongue; but in deed (action) and in truth" (1 John 3: 18).

- Be patient, kind, humble, fair, just, and slow to anger (1 Corinthians 13:4-5).

- Rejoice in what is true but do not: envy, have high opinion of yourself, keep account of evil, or take pleasure in wrong doing (1 Corinthians 13:6).

- Exercise your power to undergo all things, remain faithful and hopeful in all things (1 Corinthians 13:7).

- Have unfailing and unconditional love like God (1 Corinthians 13:8, 13; Jeremiah 31:3).

Finally, "Beloved, if God so loved us, we ought also to love one another. No man hath seen God at any time. If we love one another, God dwelleth in us, and his love is perfected in us. Hereby know we that we dwell in him, and he in us, because he hath given us of his Spirit. And we have seen and do testify that the Father sent the Son to be the Saviour of the world. Whosoever shall confess that Jesus is the Son of God, God dwelleth in him, and he in God. And we have known and believed the love that God hath to us. God is love; and he that dwelleth in love dwelleth in God, and God in him. Herein is our love made perfect, that we may have boldness in the Day of Judgment: because as he is, so are we in this world. There is no fear in love; but perfect love casteth out fear: because fear hath torment. He that feareth is not made perfect in love. We love him, because he first loved us" (1 John 4:11-19).

Thank you for sharing this journey with me. I truly pray God's love and power may be fully manifested in your life and mine, and that this book points us to the One who can provide help and hope for the journey.

May God bless you, my fellow pilgrim.

> "Give diligence to make your calling and election sure: for if ye *do these things*, ye shall never fall"
> (2 Peter 1:10).

## REFLECTION NOTES

# REFLECTION NOTES

# REFLECTION NOTES

# REFLECTION NOTES

# REFLECTION NOTES

# REFLECTION NOTES

# RECOMMENDED RESOURCES

**From Sailor to Saint**

The Navy was his life... but God did not leave it to Chance. Randrick Chance joined the US Navy to see the world. In a few short years, his naval career was thriving as he earned promotion after promotion. But as the lure of success beckoned Chance, so did God. This inspiring book chronicles his journey in discovering God, how he found true peace and purpose, and how you can find it too. Chance has travelled to over 20 countries and lives in Huntsville, Alabama with his Beautiful Marvelous Wife (BMW), Rhonitta. **$11.99**

**The Certainty of God's Promises**

In these turbulent economic times coupled with constant natural disasters, where do you turn for hope and peace? Do you need a sure word to stand on? Do you need *certainty*? Would assurance straight from God help? Then it's time you discovered *The Certainty of God's Promises*. This book is a MUST read if you want to take your life to the next level. It reveals: Why God cannot lie; How to claim His Promises; How to grow your faith; How to receive large blessings; and more. **$5.99**

# Recommended Resources

**Coming Soon! Coming Soon!**

If you truly want wall-to-wall happiness and success, in your home and in your marriage, then this book is for you. If you are married, single, engaged, thinking of marriage, separated, divorced, or in a love relationship, then this book is for you! In this timely and eagerly anticipated book, US Navy veteran, author, speaker, missionary, and life coach, Randrick Chance, shares vital *Marriage Principles* with you. This book will transform your marriage and life for the better and make your family a blessing to society. In his candid format, Chance shows you how to have and keep love, joy, peace, and marital bliss – everything you expected when you first said, "*I do*."

Are you living up to the full potentials God intends for you? Have you settled for a few paltry achievements the world calls "success?" What if God's definition and methods of success were completely opposite of your view of success? This inspirational book is the last book you will ever need to read about achieving success and reaching your goals. It paints heaven's view of successful living from a biblical perspective and shows you exactly how to have and become a success. Prepare yourself for God's best as you study His Principles of Successful Christian Living.

## Five Ways to Order:

1. Amazon.com
2. Amiarealchristian.com
3. Barnesandnoble.com
4. Strategicsecrets.com
5. 7smr.org

*A US Veteran and Christian owned Business.*

www.ingramcontent.com/pod-product-compliance
Lightning Source LLC
Chambersburg PA
CBHW020012050426
42450CB00005B/430